Examining the impact of sport throughout the American West, the series takes on the hard questions. In particular it seeks to illuminate how sport intersects historically with such cultural issues as race, ethnicity, gender, and class. By bringing engaging stories into sharper focus through little-examined or recovered sources, the series aims to engage and enlighten a wide-ranging fan base.

ALSO IN THE SPORT IN THE AMERICAN WEST SERIES

Our White Boy by Jerry Craft with Kathleen Sullivan

PLAYING IN SHADOWS

Playing in Shadows

TEXAS AND NEGRO LEAGUE BASEBALL

Rob Fink
Foreword by Cary D. Wintz

TEXAS TECH UNIVERSITY PRESS

This book is typeset in Scala. The paper used in this book meets the minimum requirements of ANSI/NISO Z39.48–1992 (R1997). ∞

Designed by Lindsay Starr

Library of Congress Cataloging-in-Publication Data
Fink, Rob (Robert)
    Playing in shadows : Texas and Negro league baseball / Rob Fink ; foreword by Cary D. Wintz.
        p. cm.
    Includes bibliographical references and index.
    Summary: "Offers the first book-length history of the Texas Negro Leagues and the impact African American Texans had on baseball during the first half of the twentieth century. Previously untold historical narrative contributes to sport history studies while asserting Texas's role in the formation, growth, and decline of African American baseball"—Provided by publisher.
    ISBN 978-0-89672-701-4 (hardcover : alk. paper) 1. Negro leagues—Texas—History. 2. Basebal—Texas—History. 3. Baseball players—Texas—History. 4. African American baseball players—Texas—History. I. Title.
    GV863.T42T495 2010
    796.357'640973--dc22   2009044286

PRINTED IN THE UNITED STATES OF AMERICA
10   11   12   13   14   15   16   17   18 / 9 8 7 6 5 4 3 2 1

TEXAS TECH UNIVERSITY PRESS
Box 41037, Lubbock, Texas 79409–1037 USA
800.832.4042 | ttup@ttu.edu | www.ttup.ttu.edu

For Tiffany, Andrew, and Dylan
With love

Contents

Illustrations

Foreword

Baseball is as American as apple pie. The game itself, which evolved out of a variety of bat and ball games in the mid-nineteenth century, is woven symbolically into American history. The myth of its origins ascribes Abner Doubleday as its creator and Cooperstown, New York, 1839, as its place and date of birth. Doubleday, who was a West Point graduate and served with honor in the Mexican War and the Civil War, makes a fitting inventor of the American pastime. However, baseball is not always as it seems. Research debunks the Doubleday-Cooperstown myth, but fails to identify the game's originator. Baseball emerged from the polyglot that was mid-nineteenth-century America. Distinctly American, its heritage includes a variety of European and American sources, dating back into the Middle Ages. The game as we know it developed among the baseball clubs in the New York City area, who in the mid-1840s codified the first known set of baseball rules. Although this process did not involve Doubleday, the Civil War and Reconstruction, with their movement of troops and prisoners, did help spread the game and its rules throughout the country.

In the post–Civil War era, baseball evolved from an amateur to a professional sport. In 1857 sixteen amateur teams in the New York area created the National Association of Base Ball Players (NABBP). By the end of the

Civil War there were more than one hundred affiliated baseball clubs. Two years later that number had doubled. In December 1868 the NABBP created a professional category of teams. A few months later the Cincinnati Red Stockings organized as the first professional baseball team. In 1871 the first baseball major league was formed and operated for four years. In 1875 the current National League was founded. Its policies transferred power from the players to the teams by controlling who could play for whom. It also set up a regular schedule of games that all league teams followed. In 1901 the American League emerged as the second major league. A year later leaders of the two major leagues and representatives of the association of other professional leagues negotiated an agreement regularizing relations among the various baseball leagues. This agreement gave the teams control over players through a rigid contract system, established the World Series between the two major leagues, and codified the dominance of the two major leagues over the other, minor, leagues. The structure of the two eight-team major leagues remained essentially unchanged for more than half a century.

Baseball appeared in Texas immediately after the Civil War. As professional teams emerged, the premier professional league in the state, the Texas League, began operation in 1888. For anyone growing up in Texas from the early years of the twentieth century through the mid-1950s, baseball *was* the Texas League. During its heyday, the league comprised seven teams, two of which were in Oklahoma. Reflecting the mores of the region, the Texas League was segregated.

To view baseball as merely a boys' game played by men ignores the deep connections between baseball and American society as well as the complexity of organized baseball. Baseball was a business, and players were commodities sold by minor league clubs to the majors and traded or sold from one major league club to another. Under the reserve clause that became standard at the end of the nineteenth century, players were contractually bound to the team that signed them. They had no voice about trades or the selling of their contracts. They were not slaves—they were always free to quit the game. But, as long as they remained in organized baseball, they had little control over their own careers. Baseball, though, was more than a business. Baseball, as the national pastime, united the country in a common activity and built local identity and pride. It was both a vehicle for the Americanization of the immigrants and a lens that brought into sharp focus the ugly power of race and racial prejudice.

Baseball served as an engine of Americanization as one ethnic minority after another sent its youth to play the game. In the process they produced a series of national heroes. For example, the Irish gave the game Connie Mack; the Poles, Stan "The Man" Musial; the Germans, the great Lou Gehrig; the Italians, of course, Joe DiMaggio; and the Jews, Hank Greenberg. The fame of these men, and many others, transcended their ethnic origins. This tradition was baseball at its best—Americans, mostly of the laboring classes, acquiring fame and some fortune (if not professional freedom). Regardless of their ethnic background, they were celebrated locally and nationally, their exploits featured in newspapers and later radio broadcasts, and children of all classes collected their baseball cards, adorned their bedrooms with their photographs, and dreamed of being baseball stars themselves. There was one problem with this picture of democracy—no blacks need apply.

Jim Crow was a part of baseball from the beginning. Of course segregation was part of America, too, and racial boundaries became more rigid in the late nineteenth and early twentieth centuries, the very years in which baseball became the national pastime. At least to some degree, all-white baseball teams simply reflected racial mores of turn-of-the-century America. Yet the color line in baseball appeared earlier and was in some ways more rigid than in other forms of segregation. The first effort to ban black players from playing on white teams occurred during Reconstruction. Informally teams began to ban black players. Also, some white players refused to play against black players. A more formal example occurred in 1867 when the all-black Camden, New Jersey, Pythians were denied affiliation with the NABBP. That organization voted to exclude any baseball club that had a black player. Ironically this decision was made just as the Fourteenth Amendment to the U.S. Constitution was being ratified by the states.

In the nineteenth century, racial barriers in baseball remained slightly porous. At least thirteen and perhaps as many as thirty-three African Americans played on supposedly white teams in the 1870s and 1880s. Most notable were Bud Fowler, who signed with a minor league team in Lynn, Massachusetts, in 1878, becoming the first black professional baseball player, and Moses Fleetwood Walker, who in 1884 became the first African American to play in the major leagues. In 1885 a gentlemen's agreement among owners and officials of the various leagues eliminated black players from white teams. This move was supported by white players, a number of whom refused to play with or against black players. A few blacks got around the rule by playing as Indians or Hispanics, but by the end of the century there were no black players in the major leagues or in the upper levels of the minor leagues.

Excluded from white baseball, African Americans formed their own baseball teams and leagues. The first of many teams was the Cuban Giants, an all-black team organized in Brooklyn in 1884. Initially these teams barnstormed, scheduling games whenever and wherever they could. While teams had their home fields and a regular season of sorts, they often traveled great distances, scheduling games against local black (and often white) teams, or scheduling exhibitions with other traveling black teams. Early efforts at creating formal leagues were generally short lived until the post–World War I era, when the black migration established a large and stable fan base in northern cities. Rube Foster, who broke in with the Waco, Texas, Yellow Jackets, and then starred as a pitcher on a number of northern teams, organized the National Negro League, the most successful of the African American major leagues, in 1920. Two years later the Eastern Colored League was born, and the two black major leagues instituted a black World Series. The onset of the Great Depression and the untimely death of Foster in 1930 undermined these leagues, but black baseball continued through hard times, bolstered by the rich pool of African American baseball talent. Segregation sustained black baseball into the 1940s.

In 1947 Jackie Robinson opened the baseball season playing first base for the Brooklyn Dodgers. This event shattered the color line in major league baseball and was the beginning of the end of the Negro baseball leagues. The movement to sign talented African American baseball players began in the early 1940s. Several baseball owners began scouting talent in the Negro leagues. These early plans to sign black players or integrate teams were firmly blocked by baseball commissioner Kenesaw Mountain Landis, an ardent racist and segregationist who presided over baseball from 1920 until his death in 1944. With the passing of Landis, Brooklyn Dodgers president and general manager Branch Rickey signed Jackie Robinson to a contract in October 1945. The following year Rickey signed four other black players, as did several other teams. The second team to desegregate, the Cleveland Indians, brought Larry Doby to the majors on July 5, 1947. Other teams followed, but slowly. By 1953 only six teams had black players. The last team to integrate was the Boston Red Sox in 1959.

Baseball, which was at the forefront of segregation in the late nine-teenth century, was again at the forefront as desegregation spread in the mid-twentieth century. Jackie Robinson challenged baseball's color line be-fore President Truman embraced civil rights in the 1948 election campaign, before the *Brown* decision that began the desegregation of public schools, before the Montgomery bus boycott and the rise of Martin Luther King, before the civil rights acts of the 1950s and 1960s and the marches and sit-ins of the 1960s. Baseball impacted the Jim Crow system in a variety of contexts. The signing of Robinson and other black baseball stars to con-tracts accelerated the desegregation of the minor leagues. Robinson spent 1946 on the Dodgers' minor league team in Montreal, and played games in a number of northern cities and southern cities. In 1952 the Dallas Eagles desegregated the Texas League. The following year the Milwaukee Braves assigned nineteen-year-old Hank Aaron to their Jacksonville team of the all-white South Atlantic (Sallie) League. Aaron was a star in the league, but he endured constant racial taunts and threats of violence. This treatment, along with the hostility of many of their teammates, was faced by countless black players as they joined white teams and leagues in the late 1940s and 1950s. Much of this hostility would fade as integrated teams achieved suc-cess on the playing field. But, some remained, as Hank Aaron experienced in 1974 as he approached Babe Ruth's home-run record.

Beyond desegregating teams and leagues, baseball played another, less visible role in the dismantling of Jim Crow. On October 17, 1960, Houston was awarded a major league franchise. This was the first franchise awarded to a city in the former Confederate states, and in the franchise negotia-tions Houston guaranteed that its baseball stadium would be completely desegregated. Before the team played its first game in April 1962, the city recognized that major league baseball could not function in a city with seg-regated hotels, restaurants, and other public spaces. Quietly and quickly, Houston desegregated these facilities.

Baseball, which for years had reflected American apartheid, assumed a significant role in breaking down racial separation. The youth of Amer-ica posted on their walls pictures of new heroes—Jackie Robinson, Willie Mays, Hank Aaron. Sadly, though, early black stars were denied this recog-nition, and with desegregation memories of their exploits and of the Negro leagues faded. The Negro leagues themselves quickly disappeared. The

National Negro League dismantled after the 1948 season, although some teams continued playing for a time. The American Negro League struggled on as a minor league until 1958.

In the recent past historians and baseball scholars have attempted to research, preserve, and analyze African American baseball and the Negro baseball teams and leagues. The National Baseball Hall of Fame at Cooperstown has identified and inducted Negro League stars, and the Negro Leagues Baseball Museum opened in Kansas City in 1990. Despite these efforts and the appearance of a number of books on the subject, much of the detailed history of the leagues remains unknown. The scarcity of historical data and sources documenting the day-to-day activities keeps black baseball in the shadows.

In his study of African American Texans and the Negro leagues, Rob Fink adds significantly to our understanding of black baseball during the first half of the twentieth century. He provides the most comprehensive study to date of black baseball in Texas. He traces this history from its roots in semiprofessional baseball, to a discussion of organized professional leagues, especially the Texas-Oklahoma-Louisiana League at the end of the 1920s, and finally to the brief run of the Houston Eagles in the waning days of the Negro National League. Fink also clearly establishes the role of Texas blacks in the Negro major leagues—most notably Rube Foster, who began his career playing Texas semipro baseball, moved to a Chicago team, became a team owner, and in 1920 organized the Negro National League, but also other Texans who contributed, mostly as players.

Fink's most significant contribution, however, is his imaginative use of the limited sources available to him, especially his close examination of the major Texas black newspapers from the 1920s through the 1940s. Although these papers did not cover black baseball consistently or systematically, the more than fifty articles he found provide valuable information. Also key are the oral history interviews that he consulted or conducted himself and autobiographical writings of black ballplayers in Texas that he uncovered. These are twice enriching, first in the detail they add to this story, and second in how they inform Fink's reading of previously published materials. What is accomplished here reminds us what is always to be gained from close scrutiny of even the most limited primary and secondary sources. Ultimately, however, *Playing in Shadows*'s enduring value may be measured in its ongoing contribution to recovery and preservation, that is, in the way it brings additional information to light from families, fans, and anyone who has collected materials on black baseball in Texas.

CARY D. WINTZ
Houston, Texas

Preface

For most Americans, the history of the Negro leagues did not exist until 1970. That year Robert Peterson published his groundbreaking book, *Only the Ball Was White*. The following year Leroy "Satchel" Paige became the first player from the Negro leagues inducted into the National Baseball Hall of Fame in Cooperstown, New York. Over the next three decades, historians and fans researched and steadily pieced together a forgotten part of baseball history.

I have always been a fan of baseball and baseball history. I knew of the Negro leagues and their most famous players but not the in-depth, vibrant history of the game. The moment of inspiration for me came while listening to Buck O'Neil in Ken Burns's documentary *Baseball*. O'Neil presented such a wonderful narrative of his experiences that I decided to study the topic more. Through my research a theme emerged concerning the important role Texas and black Texans played in shaping the Negro leagues and all of baseball. These outstanding teams, players, and leagues had remained virtually absent from the historical record. As a result, I felt a commission to bring them out of the shadows.

In writing this book I have accumulated a long list of people to whom I am eternally grateful. I must first and foremost thank Judith Keeling and

Texas Tech University Press for giving me the opportunity to tell an important part of history. Furthermore, I want to thank Alwyn Barr and Jim Harper. Their guidance and encouragement helped get this project off the ground.

Numerous other people and groups also deserve recognition for the assistance they gave me in completing the fact-finding part of this project. I will never be able to express the gratitude I feel toward George Forkerway for allowing me to enter his home and discuss his baseball career with him. The staff of the Southwest Collection at Texas Tech University, especially Randy Vance, Monte Monroe, Tai Kreidler, and Jennifer Spurrier, were invaluable during my countless hours of research. Tom Smith with the Legends of the Game Museum at the Ballpark in Arlington, the T.L.L. Temple Memorial Library in Diboll, Texas, and the Dallas/Texas Collection at the Dallas Public Library all provided important assistance and information. More thanks go to the National Baseball Hall of Fame in Cooperstown, New York, and the Negro Leagues Baseball Museum in Kansas City, Missouri, for their help, especially in acquiring pictures for the book.

I am also indebted to friends and family members who helped me over the years as I completed this book. David Robertson, John and Louise Hopper, and Dinah and Curby Ligon deserve special recognition for opening their homes to me during research trips. My parents, Bob and Trina Fink, graciously shared travel expenses and driving times, and my brother, Jon Fink, offered critical advice and encouragement along the way.

Most importantly, I extend my thanks and love to my wife, Tiffany, and sons, Andrew and Dylan. Tiffany has been my love, inspiration, and partner throughout graduate classes, comprehensive exams, oral exams, dissertations, numerous research trips, and late nights of writing. To have her beautiful face smiling next to me in the many archives has made this one of the most enjoyable experiences of my life.

My sons, Andrew and Dylan, are two of the greatest things that have ever happened to me. Their unconditional love, infectious happiness, and joyful smiles make every day bright and wonderful. It is thanks to them that I have the title of "Daddy," the designation that I am most proud of. Through the love, support, motivation, assistance, and laughter of Tiffany, Andrew, and Dylan, all my dreams become realities.

PLAYING IN SHADOWS

Life in the Shadows

1   For centuries people have made a game out of hitting a ball with some form of a bat. These games of ball took on many different forms, with no common rules. American baseball grew primarily from the English games of rounders and cricket, but other, less formal games of ball and bat also influenced baseball. Frederick Douglass recalled Southern slaves participating in ball games as both spectators and competitors.[1] At the same time, sports played a major role in the development of a distinctive African American culture and racial pride. Slaves in the American South competed in sporting events, including races, boxing matches, and ball playing, as ways to celebrate special holidays and events, such as Christmas, Easter, and weddings.[2] The opportunity to go fishing and hunting on Saturday afternoons provided a temporary release from the stress of work.[3]

Slave children also used sports as forms of cultural expression despite the dehumanizing effect of slavery. Participation in games of ball and bat, as well as other sports contests like tag, hide-and-seek, races, and Annie Over, allowed children to learn the rules of their parents' world. At the same time, sports and games allowed African Americans to pass on their distinctive culture from one generation to the next.[4]

Out of this diverse background that included the games of rounders and cricket, as well as other games of ball and bat played by many racial and ethnic groups in the United States, including African Americans, the American pastime of baseball developed. On September 23, 1845, twenty-eight men from New York City got together and formed the New York Knickerbocker Base Ball Club. Led by a shipping clerk named Alexander Joy Cartwright, the Knickerbockers outlined the basic rules and regulations of the game, including such standards as the diamond shape of the infield, distances between bases, how many balls and strikes a batter received, and the ways in which a batter could be gotten out.[5]

With the rules of the game set up, the Knickerbockers then looked to find competitors. On June 19, 1846, they found one, a newly created team of men, also from New York City, called the New York Base Ball Club. The two teams met at the Elysian Fields in Hoboken, New Jersey, and played the first official game of baseball.[6]

The game, using the "New York Rules" created by the Knickerbockers, spread rapidly throughout the country. Teams appeared in almost every city and town from coast to coast. Colleges sported teams. Women and African Americans also created their own clubs. With the large number of teams playing baseball, a governing body appeared in 1858 to manage the situation. The National Association of Base Ball Players (NABBP) settled disputes between teams, enforced standard rules, and decided which teams received membership in the association. The NABBP also established a practice of segregation that would last for nearly a hundred years when the association refused membership to the Philadelphia Pythians, an African American team.[7] Formed in 1869, and named for an African American fraternal organization, the Pythians played well and consistently recorded winning seasons during the late 1860s and 1870s. Still, the team was denied membership in the Pennsylvania Base Ball Association in 1867.[8]

The history of baseball in Texas parallels the national evolution of the game. The most popular legend on the origin of baseball credits Abner Doubleday with inventing the game in Cooperstown, New York, in 1839. Doubleday, a West Point graduate and an officer in the U.S. Army during the Mexican War and Civil War, was in charge of the federal troops in Galveston during Reconstruction, as well as the head of the Texas branch of the Freedmen's Bureau. Legends also credit him with bringing baseball to Texas in 1867. While the legends are appealing, baseball games had taken place in Texas before this date. By 1866–67, middle-class white Texans who had attended college in the East held informal baseball games in conjunction with holiday celebrations.[9]

The first organized baseball team in Texas appeared in 1869. Called the Bexars, the team began as a sporting club for German Americans in San Antonio and Bexar County. The first officially recognized baseball game in Texas, though, occurred two years before on April 21, 1867, in Galveston between the R. E. Lees and a team from Houston named the Stonewalls. The Stonewalls prevailed in the contest, 35–2.[10] In these early games, the level of segregation in national baseball, as in all of society, varied greatly, but in general, in Texas African Americans found themselves denied the opportunity to compete.

Segregation in baseball continued, and increased, when the sport became professional. The first professional baseball team, the Cincinnati Red Stockings, began play in 1869. The team, all of whose members were paid, did not lose a game for more than a year.[11] The success of the Red Stockings led other teams to hire players in an effort to field winning squads. Eventually, the first professional league, the National Association of Professional Base Ball Players (NAPBBP), was formed in 1871. The league lasted until 1876, when the National League replaced it. Another professional league, the American Baseball Association, began play in 1882. The American Association failed to last through the turn of the century, but the National League has continued up through the present day.[12]

Professional baseball came to Texas in 1877 when a touring team from Indianapolis traveled to Galveston as a part of a tour of the South. Later in 1884, Samuel L. Hain from Houston created Texas's first league, the Texas League. The original league operated on an amateur or semiprofessional level, but in 1887, John J. McCloskey created the all-professional Texas League. McCloskey's league, a minor league, served as the premier white league in the state, and lasts up through the present day. McCloskey's Texas League continued the system of segregation that existed both in Texas and the national baseball system.[13]

While Texas and the majority of the professional leagues and teams in the country excluded black ballplayers, a few African Americans did make it onto professional rosters during the 1880s, mostly in the northern minor leagues. Moses Fleetwood Walker made it all the way, becoming the first African American to play major league baseball as a member of the Toledo

Blue Stockings. Walker played with Toledo in the American Association during the 1884 season. His presence on the field stirred protests and anger among many of the white players on other teams, as well as among fans. As a result, Toledo released Walker in 1885 after he cracked a rib. With Walker's release, the owners of all the white professional teams in the country entered into an unofficial "gentlemen's agreement" not to sign any African Americans.[14]

With segregation solidly in place in Texas and the United States, a growing group of African American leaders throughout the country worked to promote racial pride, as well as raise the intellectual, physical, and moral images of their communities. These reformers faced considerable challenges from white society, which, regardless of black accomplishments, refused to accept African Americans strictly because of the color of their skin. At the same time, contemporary science placed considerable emphasis on measuring, classifying, and ranking human beings based on physical size. Racists throughout the country used this evidence to declare African Americans inferior to whites. Especially during the late 1800s and the first two decades of the 1900s, white society quoted "scientific fact" to degrade African Americans' physical and intellectual ability, as well as moral standing and masculinity. The "facts" were also used to make segregation in sports acceptable by "proving" African Americans less able to compete than whites. For example, the Texas State Medical Association stated in 1882 that African Americans' lungs were "lighter and smaller in cubic size" than whites, and thus black athletes were not as fit as white athletes.[15] Concepts of race changed throughout American history depending on time, place, and situation. During the first half of the twentieth century, though, when African American baseball reached its peak, scientific racism focused on skin color and ethnic origin played a part in segregation in sports.

The denigration of black masculinity played a considerable role in the sports world. By the late nineteenth century, male gender identity was expressed and defined solidly through sports. Among whites, images of strength and virility transcended social class and ethnic divisions to promote a positive image of white males. While black athletes like Jack Johnson in boxing and Paul Robeson in football were able to compete in interracial events, they proved the exception to the national practice of exclusion. By denying African Americans the opportunity to compete in sports against whites, African American masculinity was also denied and black males were further presented as inferior to whites.[16]

With the system of segregation solidly in place in American society, as well as in baseball, African Americans focused on creating their own teams and leagues outside the control of whites. In 1885, the first black professional team, the Cuban Giants, appeared. The team consisted of some of the best black baseball players in the country, assembled by Frank P. Thompson. An accomplished head waiter, Thompson traveled among hotels in America, ranging from New York to Florida, depending on the season. Thompson first assembled his team in Philadelphia, then brought the players to work under him at the Argyle Hotel in Babylon, Long Island, as well as play baseball. By the end of the season, Thompson brought in more players from other semiprofessional black baseball teams to create a formidable professional touring team.[17]

Most African American baseball players joined one of the hundreds of semiprofessional black teams that formed throughout the country. The first black team to compete in Texas is unknown, but records do exist of the Galveston Flyaways who competed in the 1880s, as well as of an African American team from Dallas who faced an integrated Oberlin College team in 1888.[18] As the country entered the twentieth century, these all-black teams allowed African Americans to establish their own legacy in baseball.

African American baseball teams developed a large following. The attendance figures for games fluctuated between several hundred and several thousand depending on the time, place, and situation, but focusing on the attendance figures dilutes the importance of the games. Reports on games usually passed through informal, oral networks. While economics and other factors might have prevented regular attendance, the fans still followed the teams. The players became superstars within the black community, equally popular to the white players in the major leagues. For more than fifty years, black baseball teams worked within segregation to lift the spirits of African Americans. That the black community found a positive identity in the baseball teams is evidenced by surviving accounts that stress the passion and excitement of the fans. African Americans used sports to celebrate their community and to challenge the racial stereotypes presented by segregation. Fisk University, a historically black college in Nashville, stated in its 1889–90 catalog that physical athletics developed "sound, vigorous, evenly balanced, strong, and graceful bodies that shall be efficient instruments for the use of well-trained minds in the hard work and stern conflicts of life."[19]

The segregation in baseball was similar to that in other aspects of society. As in education, black teams never received the financial support that

white teams did. African American stars were excluded from the same restaurants and hotels as other African Americans in the United States. Black
college football teams in the South found themselves denied the opportunity to compete against the white teams in the states. African Americans
throughout the country were refused their basic rights as citizens, such
as the right to vote. Yet while segregation was not universal, it existed in
such a wide array of forms throughout the country that general segregation
proved a common feature in black life and society, and not unique to the
sport of baseball. Studying African American baseball gives one a better
understanding of the situation of segregation in the United States.

However, much of this history has been lost. Black newspapers, such
as the weekly *Houston Informer*, which began publishing in 1919, covered
African American baseball games sporadically. Because of meager budgets,
sports reporting was rarely a focus of the black press, especially during the
early twentieth century. What information black newspapers recorded usually appeared in the form of box scores that referred to players only by their
last names or nicknames. The box scores also ignored semiprofessional
teams in smaller communities, like the Abilene Black Eagles or the Lubbock Black Hubbers, in favor of more prominent teams from larger cities,
such as the Houston Black Buffaloes and the Dallas Black Giants. At the
same time, the fact that the African American newspapers in Texas covered
black baseball at all shows the sport's importance to the community.

White newspapers rarely paid any attention to black baseball games.
Occasionally, in larger northern cities such as Chicago, an important game
between two top African American teams might be reported. In smaller
towns, and especially in southern states like Texas, Negro League games
failed to make the pages of the white press. Furthermore, the majority of
the athletes who played on African American teams passed away without
notice. Gone are the memories, and even the full names, of athletes like
"Black Tank" Stewart, a talented pitcher for the Austin Black Senators. Little is even known of the players who competed in the professional Negro
leagues. Much of the history of players like "Smokey" Joe Williams and "Biz"
Mackey comes from stories passed down through other Negro League players. Most of these stories were recorded in the 1970s by historians like Robert Peterson and John Holway. Recent histories use the sources collected by
the earlier historians. As the former Negro leaguers have passed away, the
opportunity to expand the base of knowledge has passed with them. Profes-

sional archives throughout the country lack resources on teams that existed in their own cities. The Negro League Baseball Hall of Fame in Kansas City and the National Baseball Hall of Fame in Cooperstown contain information only on the prominent professional Negro leagues, players, and teams. As a result, major chapters from the history of black baseball in America have been ignored completely.

For a complete picture of African American baseball during the period of segregation, the role Texas and black Texans played in shaping the game must be examined. The history of the sport in Texas mirrored the growth and major changes that took place in Negro League baseball throughout the country. At the same time, Texas possessed such a vibrant black baseball community during the first half of the twentieth century that African American baseball in Texas played a significant part in shaping both the history of the Negro leagues and the game of baseball as a whole. Moreover, black baseball was a major force in defining the African American community in Texas, helping establish its culture and racial pride.

The foundation of African American baseball in Texas lay in the long tradition of semiprofessional black teams in the state. Black semiprofessional baseball encompassed a wide spectrum of teams and talent. Into this category fell teams such as the Houston Postoffice Carriers, who played only in the Houston City League, and the Dallas Black Giants, who played other black Texas teams and competed against professional African American teams throughout the country.

These semiprofessional teams shared many characteristics, though. They usually played on the same field as the local white team, and so played only once a week when the stadium was available. The main unifying trait of the black semiprofessional teams was that they made enough money to just cover team expenses. The players participated because they enjoyed baseball, working other jobs to provide for themselves and their families. Through these teams many black Texans became exposed to Negro League baseball and many players honed the skills they took with them to professional black teams. These local teams were significant sources of community pride and cultural expression, as well as central institutions for Texas African American communities.

From this foundation of black semiprofessional teams, the entire history of African American baseball in Texas arose. One man, Andrew "Rube" Foster, went from the semiprofessional ranks in Texas to become nationally the most influential person in all of African American baseball. From 1900 to 1930, Foster ruled the world of black baseball. Born in Calvert, Texas, in 1879, he began his baseball career as a fireball pitcher with the Waco Yellow Jackets. Foster soon left Texas and joined the Leland Giants of Chicago, where he became the most recognizable player in all of black baseball. He used his prominence to gain control of the Leland Giants, changing the name to the Chicago American Giants. He then signed away star players from other black professional teams. As a result, the American Giants became the dominant black team of the 1910s and 1920s.

Foster's greatest accomplishment and biggest impact on the Negro leagues and the game of baseball occurred in 1920 when he formed the Negro National League, the first black national professional league. Through the league, he promoted black baseball throughout the United States, including Texas, where he had all of the teams in his league conduct their spring training. Foster ran his league until 1926. He served as a physical embodiment of African American masculinity and provided black Texans with a connection to the national black culture and community.

Foster's accomplishments as a player and businessman received considerable coverage in both the Texas and national black press. At a time when white newspapers and culture used sports to affirm white masculinity, African American newspapers followed a similar pattern to present a case for black masculinity. In the press, as well as through word of mouth, African Americans used the same parameters as whites—physical size, "intelligence" as a player, the velocity a pitcher threw the ball, or the distance or power with which a batter hit the ball—to present African American masculinity. As these characteristics widely circulated throughout the country, Foster and other players achieved a status as symbols of black masculinity similar to that reached by boxer Jack Johnson during the same period. This racial definition for Foster proved especially strong in Texas, where his accomplishments were widely known.

Other players from Texas went on to national prominence in black baseball. Building on the reputation and image created by Foster, these players greatly influenced baseball and defined their positions, while serving as examples of black masculinity and furthering the reputation of the African American community, as well as black baseball, in Texas. One such Texan, "Smokey" Joe Williams, a fastball pitcher from San Antonio, pitched into his fifties and earned the distinction as the best black pitcher ever. He compiled a record of twenty-two wins, seven losses, and one tie in exhibition games against white pitchers from the major leagues. In competing against pitchers, both black and white, who eventually received induction into the National Baseball Hall of Fame, Williams posted a record of eight wins, two loses, and one tie, defeating such prominent pitchers as Christy Mathewson and Walter Johnson.[20]

Willie Wells, a slick-fielding shortstop from Austin, defined his position for twenty years in the Negro leagues. As well as being the best shortstop in the country from the 1920s to the 1930s, Wells also left his mark on the game as the inventor of the batting helmet. Historians consider Louis Santop the first great power hitter, while Raleigh "Biz" Mackey, who taught a young Roy Campanella, receives recognition as the best defensive catcher in black baseball. These players, and others, changed how baseball was played, excelled against white competition, refuting "scientific" racist claims, and increased the national reputation of black baseball in Texas.

On the basis of the state's star players, African American baseball in Texas reached its peak of influence and national prominence in the late 1920s and early 1930s. From 1929 to 1931, Texas had its own black professional league, a source of significant community pride and identity for black Texans. The league, which began as the Texas-Oklahoma-Louisiana League, formed during the beginning of the Great Depression. Despite this formidable opponent, the league managed to survive for three years and served to further legitimize African American baseball in Texas. The TOL brought several innovations to Texas baseball, such as the use of lights for night games. Before the league closed in 1931 because of a lack of funds, the league champion each year faced the champion of Rube Foster's Negro National League.

The Depression of the 1930s and World War II created hard times for African American baseball, as young men focused on work and the war effort instead of baseball. After the war, enthusiasm ran high to rebuild African American baseball in Texas, but in 1947 the baseball world turned upside down. Jackie Robinson began playing for the Brooklyn Dodgers. Robinson's appearance in white professional baseball marked the end of segregated baseball in America. African Americans now looked to integrated baseball as a source of community identity and racial pride. By 1949, the Negro National League no longer existed. Over the next decade, the majority of the once great African American professional teams around the country ceased to exist, as their good players joined integrated teams.

Texas also played a role in shaping the end of Negro League baseball. In 1949, the Newark Eagles, formerly of the Negro National League, moved to Houston in a last-ditch effort to survive. Despite the arrival of a professional black team, the interests of African American baseball fans in Texas had turned to the integrated major league teams. The black press in Texas also lost interest in African American baseball. While games were covered consistently enough in the black press, especially during the late 1940s, to show the high level of support from the African American community, that coverage stopped almost completely after integration, illustrating the shifting loyalties of African Americans.

After integration, every week numerous articles appeared in Texas's black newspapers, covering details of the on- and off-field activities of African American stars in the major leagues. Almost no articles appeared about the local black teams. As a result, the Houston Eagles attracted small numbers of fans, failed to make any money in Houston, and left after the 1950 season.

By 1950, the majority of the major black semiprofessional teams in Texas had also ceased to exist. At the local level, African Americans now competed on segregated amateur teams. The players on these teams received no financial compensation for playing, and the team expenses remained low, as these teams competed only locally. The ability of the semiprofessional teams to make money barnstorming practically disappeared, thus causing once-prominent semiprofessional teams like the Dallas Black Giants to disband.

The transition of support by black fans in Texas away from segregated teams mirrored what occurred at the time throughout all of the Negro leagues. With the demise of the Eagles, the role of segregated baseball in Texas in shaping the sport of baseball came to an end. Still, black Texans now in integrated baseball continued the legacy of influence on the sport set by their predecessors.

Over the next several decades, Texans watched their best black players sign with major league teams, as in the case of Ernie Banks of Dallas who became the first African American to play for the Chicago Cubs. A few all-black teams continued to play, but only on a local level. One such team, the Abilene Black Eagles, had no uniforms and played its games in a field outside the city limits that was devoid of bleachers, benches, and a backstop.[21]

At the same time in the early 1950s, the Texas minor leagues began to integrate. Dave Hoskins, the first black player for the Dallas Eagles of the Texas League, received weekly coverage in the state's African American newspapers. Black Texans rejoiced in the integrated local teams, and no complaints appeared about baseball's integration. The new equal opportunity in the sport marked the end of an era. When the all-black baseball teams closed and African American ballplayers integrated white teams, the legendary Texas teams and athletes disappeared from public consciousness. What could never be taken away, though, was the significant role African American baseball teams in Texas and black Texans had in shaping the state's African American community, as well as the Negro leagues and the game of baseball.

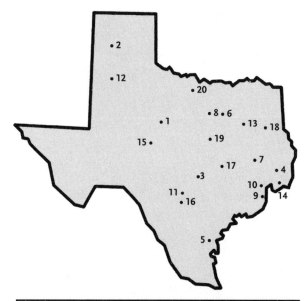

Selection of Towns That Fielded Semiprofessional African American Baseball Teams

1. Abilene	8. Fort Worth	15. San Angelo
2. Amarillo	9. Galveston	16. San Antonio
3. Austin	10. Houston	17. Taylor
4. Beaumont	11. Kerrville	18. Tyler
5. Corpus Christi	12. Lubbock	19. Waco
6. Dallas	13. Mineola	20. Wichita Falls
7. Diboll	14. Port Arthur	

Courtesy of Mike Jones

The Semiprofessional Game

THE ROOTS OF BLACK BASEBALL

2. Baseball was the dominant sport in the United States during the first half of the twentieth century. Basketball, a recent creation, existed mainly in schools and organizations such as the YMCA, filling the winter months between football and baseball seasons. Professional football was not much more than a regional sport and received little to no coverage outside the northern cities that fielded teams. The only other team sport with a national following was college football, and the fan interest in the college teams paled in comparison to interest in baseball.

Baseball's popularity as the national pastime derived from the fact that the game was played at many levels throughout the country. Professional teams, from both the major and minor leagues, dotted the map. Almost every town in America had a semiprofessional team. Religious groups, such as the House of David, even created touring teams to spread their ideals.

For African Americans, though, the world of baseball, like the rest of American society, was segregated. African Americans found themselves unable to transcend the institutional segregation, so they created their own teams and leagues that centered on sandlots and the Negro leagues. African American professional teams like the Kansas City Monarchs came to achieve the same prominence in the black community that major league teams held in the white community. Furthermore, with the migration from rural, southern areas by African Americans during the twentieth century, cities like Pittsburgh, Chicago, and Houston all developed black teams that promoted creativity, cultural expression, and community.[1]

An important aspect of segregated baseball was the sandlot game. The name "sandlot ball" referred to both the field on which games took place and the independent status of the teams, which existed outside of the control of the professional major and minor leagues.[2] Almost every town and community in the country fielded a sandlot team. Local businesses sponsored the teams but without the goal of making a profit on the games. The driving force was the opportunity for men to play ball and the African American community to gather, support its teams, and celebrate its culture.[3]

As in the rest of the country, the majority of African Americans in Texas who played baseball never made it to the professional level. Only a small minority of black baseball players participated in the professional Texas-Oklahoma-Louisiana League during its three-year existence. Instead, the experience of most black ballplayers in Texas remained limited to the semiprofessional scene that existed throughout the first half of the twentieth century. While the levels of organization and quality of talent varied greatly, what united semiprofessional black baseball and distinguished it from professional African American baseball was that no semiprofessional player made his living playing baseball. As with white semiprofessional teams, African American ballplayers received not much more than meal money and all worked other jobs, playing baseball only in their free time.[4]

In smaller towns like Diboll, the players supported the team out of their own pockets. The team members bought their own uniforms and equipment, which were then used throughout the players' tenure with the team.[5] Occasionally in the larger cities, as in the case of the Houston Postoffice Carriers, the athletes' place of employment sponsored the team. Other teams, like the Abilene Black Eagles, consisted of players selected by a prominent member of the city's black community, usually a local businessman. The players on the Black Eagles held a wide variety of jobs that had no connection to the team.[6]

If the town possessed one major industry, the bulk of the players usually worked for that company. In Diboll, almost all of the players on the Dragons semiprofessional team worked for the Southern Pine Lumber Company, yet the company had no direct relation to the team.[7] Also, at the semipro level, local youths played on the teams if they exhibited adequate ability. According to Ruben "Jellie" Samuel of the Diboll Dragons, "Herbert Allen and another one were schoolboys. We had a couple of schoolboys playing with us because they were kind of big."[8]

For African Americans living in rural regions, baseball took other forms. Crush Holloway, who was born in Hillsboro, Texas, in 1896, remembered life and baseball in the central Texas cotton community: "At sunrise we'd be in the field plowing. Oh that was big cotton. . . . I started playing baseball on the sandlots, playing every Sunday if I could get off from home. . . . All the boys would get together and play all day long Sunday, two or three different games, until the sun went down. . . . We use to make our own balls in the country: twine and wrappings."[9] Numerous semiprofessional teams in Texas appeared, thrived, fell on hard times, and disappeared, mirroring the peaks and valleys that occurred in both white baseball and professional black baseball. Since every important person in black baseball in Texas began his career in the semiprofessional ranks, black semiprofessional baseball was the foundation of the influence Texas eventually exerted on the Negro leagues and the game of baseball.

Black professional baseball offered not much of an alternative to the semiprofessional game. Similar to the early experience of black baseball players in Pittsburgh, no representative team of the major Negro leagues existed in Texas until 1949.[10] Furthermore, professional black baseball in Texas was short-lived. As a result, the semiprofessional game was a source of community identity and cultural pride.

The exact date of the first semiprofessional African American baseball game in Texas, or even the name of the first team, remains unknown. By the early 1900s, the few existing black newspapers made only occasional references to teams in Texas. The acknowledgment of these teams usually existed only as reference points in articles on the beginnings of star players in professional African American baseball, such as Rube Foster. Current games were mentioned only when the local semiprofessional teams faced one of Texas's black college teams, such an exhibition games between Prairie View A&M University and a local semiprofessional team made up of the university faculty. To establish fan recognition, African American teams usually took their names from the local white team, just adding the word "black" to the title, such as the Dallas Black Giants.

The fact that the semiprofessional teams never played a set schedule clouds the history of these African American baseball teams. The teams

picked up games wherever possible, taking on all challengers. When the
Dallas Black Giants faced the San Antonio Black Bronchos in a two-game
series during June of 1919, the contest marked the first time the two
teams had played each other in several years. The delay resulted from the
inability of the two teams to reach a game date that proved mutually acceptable.[11]

Practices, too, occurred inconsistently. In Diboll, the Dragons played on
Sundays if a game could be organized. Since most of the players worked for
the Southern Pine Lumber Company, their work schedules prevented them
from practicing during the week. As a result, their only practice took place
on Sunday mornings, just before their games began.[12]

The black teams also lacked permanent playing facilities. In large cities,
such as Austin or Houston, the black teams played in the local white stadiums at the discretion of the white teams. In the last week of August 1919,
the San Antonio Black Aces and Beaumont Black Oilers prepared to play a
four-game series in Beaumont at the local white stadium, while the white
Aces and Oilers faced each other in Galveston. The first game in Galveston
had such a low attendance that the white teams moved the remainder of
their games to Beaumont, forcing the black teams to cancel their series.[13]

The only other playing facilities available for African American teams
were substandard fields in black neighborhoods. In Dallas, the Black Giants played at Gardner Park, a baseball field that flooded so badly when it
rained that the *Dallas Express* called it "an ideal spot for fishing or yacht rac-
ing."[14] In rural areas, the teams competed in fields, usually without back-
stops, dugouts, or even benches on which to sit.[15]

Despite the problems in procuring fields, the opportunity to use white
stadiums when available gave black Texans an advantage African Americans in other parts of the country did not have. Crush Holloway credited
the success of so many black Texans in the Negro leagues to their playing in
white Texas League parks. According to Holloway, "That's why those boys
from Texas could play so good, they had good grounds. Not like out East,
where they had to play on those little lots."[16]

Black semiprofessional teams appeared and disappeared quickly, regularly changing names and players. What records that exist usually refer to
players by their last name, or in many cases, by nicknames, such as "Tank"
Stewart, a pitcher for the Austin Black Senators.[17] The reference to players
by their nicknames, though, helped promote African American masculinity.

Monikers such as "Tank" and "Crush" presented powerful, athletic, masculine images of the black males at a time when segregation and scientific racism denied African Americans equality as human beings.

At the start of the 1919 baseball season, a San Antonio team went by the name of the Black Bronchos. By August, the team had changed its name to the Black Aces.[18] When published accounts of games occurred, black newspapers ran either a box score or a small article on the game. While informative for the fans who knew the team and the players, a large part of the history has been lost. The box scores, while providing statistical information, gave only the players' last names, removing the human element from the story. The articles on the games presented exciting pictures of specific plays and events, but only a few players received recognition. As a result, the contributions of the rest disappeared. White newspapers failed to cover the African American teams. Since only a handful of black newspapers existed in Texas, the teams from the large cities received the coverage. Teams from small towns, especially those in West Texas where there was no major black newspaper, left little to no historical record. As a result, records are slim at best during the first few decades of the 1900s.

Another obstacle faced by semiprofessional baseball teams, both black and white, involved travel to out-of-town games. Semiprofessional teams were usually unable to afford a team bus or use public transportation. As a result, they traveled by car in caravan style. Ruben Samuel remembered, "Everybody who had a car would take three or four of us."[19]

By 1920, black semiprofessional baseball in Texas had started to change. Black newspapers in the state began to offer more coverage of Texas teams. Also, with a period of economic prosperity following World War I, African Americans around the country, as well as in Texas, became more interested in baseball. It was at this time in Chicago that native Texan Rube Foster created the Negro National League, the first professional black baseball league in the country.

The interest in baseball among African Americans also came from the hundreds of thousands who had moved to large cities to take advantage of jobs opened up by World War I. The black populations of cities like Chicago more than tripled during the first two decades of the 1900s. Baseball served as a unifying experience for these immigrants.[20] Those who moved to places like Pittsburgh, Chicago, Houston, and Dallas settled in all-black neighborhoods. Within these neighborhoods, black-owned businesses developed that allowed African Americans to avoid contact with whites and their prejudices.[21] In northern cities, occasionally games occurred between the black teams and local white teams, but these games always took place under terms set by the white teams. African Americans learned to work within these rules and not to challenge white ideas of black racial inferiority.[22] In Texas, no such interracial games occurred, making the separate black culture the only sphere for baseball and community expression.

Baseball throughout the country also played a role in urbanization. Team owners and journalists created a self-serving image of the sport. These men, both white and black, promoted the game as a uniquely American institution. Furthermore, they promoted baseball as the guardian and transmitter of the ideals of an older, simpler rural society. In reality, the team owners who dominated the sport all had ties to urban political machines and used these connections to promote their own business interests, as well as protect the political positions of the teams themselves.[23]

The same was true for black teams throughout the country.[24] In Texas, several African American businessmen who sponsored black baseball teams from around the state tried to create a semiprofessional league of their own. Calling it the Texas Colored Baseball League (TCL), representatives from Dallas, Fort Worth, Houston, Waco, Austin, Beaumont, Shreveport, Galveston, and San Antonio met in Fort Worth on Sunday, March 21, 1920, to determine the league's operating procedures. The men present at the meeting assigned franchises, set schedules, appointed umpires, and set roster limits. They also created a guarantee fund of one hundred dollars per team to ensure against game forfeitures.[25] The organizers believed if the teams had money invested in the league, then they would play out their season no matter what for fear of losing the hundred dollars.

Unfortunately, from the very beginning the Texas Colored League's publicity department failed to inform the public of the league's actions. No major press releases or publications went out concerning the details of the organizational meeting. Black Texans knew nothing of schedule dates or team rosters. This lapse created uncertainty among baseball fans about whether the league really existed or not, if the meeting had succeeded, and what took place. As a result, fan support for the TCL was minuscule from the very beginning.[26]

The failure to promote itself caused the Texas Colored League to suffer financially. It lost over five hundred dollars in the inaugural game between Dallas and Fort Worth because of low attendance stemming from the lack of publicity.[27] With the fear of financial failure hanging over their heads, the league directors sought to cut expenses. The directors hired schoolboys to work as official scorers, since children worked more cheaply than adults.[28] Individual teams also tried promotions to attract fans to games. In Dallas, local businesses gave out prizes at the Black Giants' games. The prizes, though, went not to fans but to the players for accomplishments on the field, such as a free shoeshine for the first player to hit a triple. The appeal of paying fifty cents to one dollar per ticket to watch a game in which prizes went only to players proved minimal. The promotions failed to bring fans to Dallas's games.[29] Despite all the problems, the league survived its first year, with Fort Worth winning the pennant.

The effort to create a black-owned baseball league in Texas was part of a larger movement by African Americans throughout the state and country to establish their own cultural and community institutions during a period of intense racial segregation. During the 1920s, African Americans created the Independent Voters League (IVL) in Texas. The IVL, a political organization, fought for issues important to the black community, such as better schools and increased African American political participation.[30] At the same time, efforts to organize African American intercollegiate sports in the state led to the creation of the Southwestern Athletic Conference (SWAC) in 1920 by six of Texas's historically black colleges.[31]

In 1921, the team owners and businessmen of the Texas Colored League met again, this time in Beaumont, and prepared for their second season of competition. At the organizational meeting, though, some changes took place. First, the team representatives cleared up debts from the previous year owed to Waco and Austin, who had dropped out of the league. Next, the league members decided to adopt a traveling umpire system, with each team playing only once a week. The fewer number of games and smaller group of umpires lowered expenditures. Furthermore, by playing only one game a week, the teams gained the opportunity to make some extra money by scheduling games against semiprofessional teams from around the state that were not part of the Texas Colored League.[32] This practice of supplementing incomes by booking nonleague games on days off was a common practice among black professional teams in the Negro National League.

The TCL members made other moves to keep costs down. The league established a limit of sixteen players per team, as well as adopted a salary cap for each team. These decisions, in theory, made the league more competitive, while also keeping salaries to a minimum. Additionally, since the one-hundred-dollar fee did not prove a strong enough deterrent to prevent the forfeiture by Waco and Austin the previous season, the deposit paid by each team guaranteeing its commitment to play the entire season increased to two hundred dollars.[33] Finally, the Texas Colored League learned from the previous season's publicity mistakes and worked to promote itself better. As the 1921 season began, with Beaumont, Dallas, Fort Worth, Galveston, Houston, and Shreveport preparing to compete, excitement in the black press and across Texas for African American baseball ran high. The level of commitment to the Texas Colored League is even more impressive considering the league was semiprofessional. Every player worked a full-time job and played baseball as a pastime, receiving only a minuscule salary.

The excitement over African American baseball in Texas extended beyond the Texas Colored League. The newly established *Houston Informer*, founded in 1919, gave weekly accounts of the Black Buffaloes' accomplishments. In March, the paper told of the team's spring training workouts under manager W. B. Patterson and the preseason exhibition games against local black colleges.[34] In East Texas, J. S. Payne, a black sports promoter from Shreveport, Louisiana, attempted to form the Tri-State Baseball League, consisting of teams from Texas, Louisiana, and Arkansas.[35] The same year, catcher Chris Spearman of the Dallas Black Giants signed to play for the Brooklyn Royal Giants, while Chaney White and Willis Rector, both also former Black Giants, joined the Philadelphia Hilldales.[36] As professional Negro League teams, the Royal Giants and Hilldales represented the pinnacle of black baseball in the United States in the early 1920s.

The Texas Colored League began the 1921 season on April 16 with a game in Dallas between the Black Giants and the Fort Worth Black Panthers. Before the game, the TCL held a large parade through the city's streets, complete with a brass band, club officials, local businessmen, and amusement concerns. At the place of honor in the parade, the players for both teams rode in automobiles escorted by two mounted policemen.[37] The parade further promoted the ties between sports and black business in segregated towns.

African American newspapers reported the games of the TCL with excitement and vivid details. The *Houston Informer* referred to a three-game series between the Black Giants and the Black Buffaloes as "the greatest games witnessed here in several years."[38] It went on to give an account of the games and describe the exploits of such players as "Coon" Pryor and "Sweetheart" Lewis. That the press referred to a player by a nickname meant that he was well known in the community. In addition to providing basic accounts of the games, newspapers also offered critiques of the teams' play. According to the *Informer*, the inability of the Black Buffaloes to execute a squeeze play "made our team look like a tore up cigar on Market Street in Philadelphia."[39]

During the early 1920s, through organizations such as the TCL, semiprofessional African American baseball in Texas established itself with fans as a dominant sport. Players, such as Fort Worth's ace pitcher, whom fans knew only by the nickname "Black Tank," became local celebrities. The newspaper articles rarely gave the players' names or detailed box scores of the games. Still, almost every week some account appeared in the *Houston Informer*, *Dallas Express*, or *San Antonio Register* that told who won the previous week and what significant plays took place.

As happened with the professional Negro leagues and white minor league baseball in Texas, fan interest and black newspaper coverage for Texas's semiprofessional African American baseball teams increased dramatically in the 1920s. One contest between the Black Buffaloes and the Fort Worth Black Panthers in 1921 drew the largest crowd to witness an African American game in Houston up to that point.[40] In 1922, Dallas recorded an average of three thousand fans a game.[41]

Like their white counterparts, the semiprofessional black teams went on tours of the state, further building up fan awareness of and excitement about African American baseball. To have Houston play against teams in Dallas, Fort Worth, and Shreveport, for example, created rivalries based around city pride. As a result, even those who weren't baseball fans became more interested in the achievements of their local team. The opportunity for black Houstonians to claim superiority over those in San Antonio, for example, made the teams an important part of community identity. Furthermore, by playing black college teams, such as Paul Quinn College in Waco, or teams from smaller towns such as Corsicana or Mexia, the more prominent teams padded their win-loss records, thus attracting casual fans who enjoyed associating themselves with successful organizations.[42]

The professional Negro League teams throughout the country also followed this pattern. Touring teams used games against semipro or college teams to scout for new talent as well as make some money. In 1920, the Indianapolis ABCs signed away six players from the San Antonio Black

Aces, including star catcher "Biz" Mackey, after facing the Black Aces during a tour of Texas.[43]

Even as semiprofessional black baseball established itself and grew in popularity in the early 1920s, the sport still experienced some problems. One problem centered on the athletes. Team rosters changed frequently, as the players switched teams for more money and a chance to play on a winning team. No regulations prevented players from jumping teams or stopped teams from signing away players. In May 1921, the Houston Black Buffaloes exhibited this trend when they signed a new starting catcher, "Georgetown" Williams, as well as a utility player named Burney, both from Prairie View University. At the same time, the Black Buffaloes saw their first baseman, "Billy Bowlegs" Curtis, sign with the Galveston Black Oilers for more money and a better job.[44] Players jumping teams affected African American baseball throughout the country, not just in Texas. The practice is exemplified in the career of Leroy "Satchel" Paige but occurred regularly at all levels of the game.

One incident of a player changing teams at the semiprofessional level in Texas involved Ruben Samuel. Samuel was playing for a team in Shreveport, Louisiana, in 1940 when the Diboll Dragons came to town for a game. As Samuel later told an interviewer, "they [Diboll] came up there to play ball and they beat us and I came on back with them to play ball with them."[45]

A major problem for black, as well as white, semiprofessional teams in Texas was sporadic attendance. One weekend series of games might draw several thousand fans. But another series might not. According to the *Houston Informer*, a three-game series in Shreveport between the Black Buffaloes and the Shreveport Black Gassers in 1921 attracted barely "enough people at the game to start a fuss with the peanut vender."[46] Homer E. McCoy, a local black businessman who served as secretary of the Black Buffaloes and formed the National Negro Business League in Houston in 1927, expressed his disappointment over the small number of ticket receipts for the Houston-Shreveport series.[47] These fluctuating attendance numbers did not hurt the individual black semiprofessional teams that much, because a touring team could keep its expenditures low by having the host team provide all of the equipment and umpires. In addition, player salaries could come from a portion of the gate receipts and be based on the size of the crowd. For a league like the Texas Colored League, though, unpredictable fan attendance proved fatal. Without the revenue from tickets, the league had no way to pay umpires, equipment bills, and player salaries. Even though the league was semiprofessional and everyone involved had other jobs, the players could not forget the promised salaries.

As the black teams in Texas improved their play, their national reputation grew, further galvanizing the state's African American community. The opportunity to measure themselves against the best teams from around the country led black Texans to look at themselves as a unified group with a commonality of baseball.

After the 1922 season, the Memphis Red Sox, champions of the Negro Southern League, came to Dallas and faced the Black Giants in a seven-game series. The Dallas black press called the series the "Battle for the Championship of Dixie."[48] Even though Memphis defeated Dallas rather handily, the Black Giants did manage to win two of the seven games, filling the Dallas community with pride.

In April of the next year, both the Wichita Red Sox and the Kansas City Monarchs, two professional black teams, came to Texas for spring training and played the majority of the Texas teams. In Houston, the two teams faced the Black Buffaloes at Scott Street Park, a new white-owned stadium at the end of the Pierce Car Line. The stadium's proximity to public transportation allowed easier access to the games for the city's African American population, who had to travel across town to attend.[49] Houston got swept in both series by their professional opponents. Despite the losses, the *Houston Informer* tried to put a positive spin on the efforts of the Black Buffaloes, saying that Houston "played a nice game in spots."[50]

An attempt to revive the Texas Colored League took place in March of 1923. Representatives from around the state met in Houston, where they elected officers, naming A. R. Pryor of Dallas as president and secretary-treasurer. The team representatives also adopted a schedule and chose the cities to participate in the circuit. Dallas, Beaumont, Fort Worth, Galveston, Houston, Shreveport, and San Antonio all received franchises based on the existing teams and large black populations in the cities.[51] Charles C. Caffey, owner of the Houston Black Buffaloes, claimed he possessed "one of the best teams that ever represented Texas on the diamond."[52]

But unequal and sporadic attendance plagued this incarnation of the league as well. In Dallas, five thousand fans turned out for a game between the Black Giants and the Galveston Black Sand Crabs, the largest crowd in the history of Riverside Park, the Black Giants' new home.[53] However, other games throughout the state drew only a few hundred spectators.

Dallas finished in first place when the season ended in August, earlier than planned. Again the Black Giants faced Memphis in the best of nine games for the "Dixie Championship." Dallas lost for the second straight year.

For the teams that made up the Texas Colored League, the cost of membership grew too great. The requirement to play all league games, pay for equipment, travel long distances, and procure facilities that met league standards created a large expense budget. With only sporadic attendance, the revenues for the teams failed to equal the expenses needed to belong to a unified league. The management of the TCL also drew its revenue from a portion of the gate receipts. Since these failed to cover team expenses, they also failed to cover league expenses. Without steady revenue, the TCL found itself unable to pay its administrators, officials, and other expenses. Finally, the problems of money and attendance proved too much for the league to handle, and the Texas Colored League dissolved at the end of the 1923 season.[54]

Even with the demise of the organized black baseball league, the teams that made up the Texas Colored League survived. These semiprofessional teams found they could operate on a smaller budget by not having to cover costs of equipment and travel that were a necessary part of belonging to a league. When not tied to a league and a set schedule, semiprofessional teams found themselves able to compete against teams from all over the state of Texas no matter the opponents' level of ability. Teams like the Houston Black Buffaloes could play against teams like the Lubbock Black Hubbers, whose ability level and financial resources prevented them from playing in the TCL. By broadening their competition base, Texas's semiprofessional African American baseball teams increased their chances of making a profit. Also, because they did not have to pay league dues, maintain professional-level equipment and uniforms, or rent a large stadium, the teams found it easier to stay afloat. As a result, semiprofessional black baseball in Texas continued to exist and to increase its fan base.[55] Texas's national reputation for top-caliber black baseball remained high, as did the role of the sport in community development and the self-image of the African American community.

The end of the organized semipro league proved advantageous to the players, too. Since the players all had full-time jobs, meeting the strict league rules about schedules had been extremely difficult. The opportunity to play baseball at leisure for fun and a few extra dollars appealed to many black Texans.

Other African American semiprofessional teams appeared across Texas during the 1920s. Usually associated with some local business or organiza-tion, these teams rarely played outside their region. In Houston, the Post-office Carriers annually fielded a team, competing against other groups within the city but also occasionally against teams from around the state. The Houston Postoffice Carriers faced the Galveston Carriers at West End Park in Houston for a "Decoration Day" contest.[56] The annual contest creat-ed a strong rivalry, with Galveston swearing "eternal vengeance" after its de-feat in 1922.[57] The Houston Postoffice Carriers also participated in charity events, such as a benefit game against the city's Colored Commercial Club to raise money for Union Hospital.[58] The involvement of these teams in the charitable events and holidays offers another illustration of the strong role black baseball played in the African American community in Texas.

The number of fans who turned out for semiprofessional games in-creased. For one game between Houston's Colored Commercial Club (CCC) and the Prairie View University faculty team, a "large and noisy crowd who cheered misplays with as much gusto as good plays" witnessed the con-test.[59] The CCC proved victorious, winning 9 to 6, but after the game, every fan in attendance, along with the players for both teams, received a com-plimentary dinner courtesy of the university. The game, which the fans watched for free, received high praise from those in attendance. Dean Rowe of Prairie View expressed his pleasure over the high level of competition, as well as the support of the fans, saying, "I have paid $1 to see many games that did not come up to the game this afternoon."[60] Rowe's sentiments ex-pressed what many Texas communities, both black and white, felt toward their respective local semiprofessional teams.

The success of local teams such as the Houston Postoffice Carriers led fans of the game to create semiprofessional black leagues situated entirely within Texas's larger cities. While the statewide Texas Colored League failed, at the local level small, semiprofessional leagues formed that operated on a smaller budget, and thus proved more capable of surviving.

In Houston, local businesses created the City Colored League of Ama-teur Baseball Teams in 1924. The six clubs played games every Saturday from May until August at local parks and baseball fields. Each team paid a ten-dollar membership fee to cover league costs, but covered their own equipment and salaries.[61] These local league games did not possess the grandeur of the Texas Colored League games, but the city league, which changed its name to the Houston Colored Amateur Baseball League, lasted for more than a decade and provided entertainment for countless numbers of African Americans in the area.

The teams represented a wide variety of local institutions like the U.S. Postal Service, as well as black-owned businesses like the Lincoln Theater, Climax Pharmacy, and Orgen Barber Shop. Sponsorship provided publicity for the businesses, and black-owned businesses were a source of pride for the African American community. While the claim cannot be verified, the *Informer* reported that Houston was the first city in America, and particularly the South, to promote organized amateur baseball for African Americans.[62]

The last half of the 1920s proved to be the high-water mark for African American baseball in Texas. Texas had established itself as a significant home of black baseball, and a number of African American players from Texas played for the best professional black teams in the country. Some of these players, like "Smokey" Joe Williams, a power pitcher from Seguin, were recognized as the best at their positions in all of black baseball. When Andrew "Rube" Foster, himself an accomplished pitcher, founded the Negro National League in 1920, he signed several Texas players. Foster also regularly brought his Chicago American Giants, along with other professional black teams, to Texas to train against the local semiprofessional teams.

The quality of black baseball in Texas was proven in August 1925 when the Houston Black Buffaloes split a six-game series in Birmingham, Alabama, against the Birmingham Black Barons of the Negro Southern League. In the series, the Black Buffaloes proved themselves the equal of their opponents at the plate, while Houston's pitchers struck out Birmingham's star hitter, "Mule" Suttles, in all four of his at-bats. According to the *Informer*, the Birmingham press called Houston "the hardest hitting team that has graced that field for some time."[63]

The popularity of these semiprofessional teams and black baseball in Texas culminated in the creation of the professional Texas-Oklahoma-Louisiana League in 1929. The TOL was a watershed for black baseball in Texas. The first three decades of the twentieth century witnessed a steady increase in baseball's popularity among African Americans in the state. The semiprofessional teams established large followings and served as symbols of community identity and racial pride. From this semiprofessional foundation, African American baseball in Texas, along with the numerous prominent black Texans who went on to play in the Negro leagues, became a part of national African American culture and identity. But even more, black baseball in Texas shaped the entire game.

Andrew "Rube" Foster, father of the Negro National
League. National Baseball Hall of Fame Library,
Cooperstown, N.Y.

Andrew "Rube" Foster

THE FATHER OF THE NEGRO LEAGUES

3 From the foundation of black semiprofessional baseball, black Texans came to shape the game throughout the country. Men who honed their skills on the playing fields of Austin and San Antonio went on to star in the Negro leagues, changing the way the game was played. As a result, African American baseball in Texas grew to national prominence.

The role black Texans played in baseball united them as a group and highlighted the abilities of the African American community. When white baseball adopted techniques or innovations used by black teams, African Americans had evidence in arguing their equality with whites as baseball players and as human beings.

Any discussion of the important African American players from the state who helped shape the game, defined the state's African American community, and served as symbols of black masculinity must begin with one man, Andrew "Rube" Foster. During the period 1900–1930, Foster was the most influential figure in African American baseball. He began his career as one of the most dominant pitchers in the game, winning fifty-four games in 1902.[1] Foster parlayed his pitching talent into a managerial and administrative position with the Chicago American Giants. He then transformed the

American Giants into the best black baseball team in America in the 1910s and early 1920s. In 1920, Foster established his most important legacy, the first all-black professional league, the Negro National League, and ran the league until he suffered a nervous breakdown in 1926. For the first part of the twentieth century, Rube Foster *was* African American baseball. Black newspapers throughout the country covered his every action. He set the standard for how teams and leagues were run. It was through his work that the Negro leagues became the national pastime for African Americans.

Foster began his baseball career in central Texas. He was born the son of a preacher in Calvert, Texas, in 1879. According to one legend, Foster organized a baseball team of local youths while still in grade school.[2] At the age of seventeen, he left Calvert and moved to Waco, Texas, where he pitched for the Waco Yellow Jackets, a black semiprofessional team.

Foster was the physical archetype of a power pitcher. He stood six feet, four inches tall and weighed more than two hundred pounds. Foster dominated opponents with his blinding fastball and "fade-away" pitch, a reverse curve that broke in on right-handed hitters and away from left-handed hitters.[3] Stories of his ability abounded. One legend concerned how Foster acquired the nickname of "Rube." Supposedly, while pitching with a semiprofessional black team in Hot Springs, Arkansas, Foster defeated the white major league Philadelphia Athletics and their Hall of Fame pitcher Rube Waddell, in an exhibition game. For defeating Waddell, Foster received the nickname "Rube beater," which was shortened to "Rube."[4] The name stuck for the remainder of his life. Such success stories carried with them an image of black prowess and physical masculinity contrary to the image presented by the white establishment at the time.

By 1902, African American baseball people all over the country knew Foster's reputation as a pitcher. Frank Leland, owner of the Chicago Union Giants, offered Foster a contract. Leland was black Chicago's first baseball entrepreneur.[5] The contract offered by Leland included carfare from Texas to Chicago, a considerable sum and an unheard-of action at the time. In his first start for the Union Giants, Foster lived up to his reputation by pitching a shutout. However, his next several starts proved unimpressive. Disappointed in his own performance, Foster quit Leland's team and returned to Texas.[6]

Even though Foster left the Union Giants, his pitching ability was considered unmatched, and upon returning to Texas he immediately received offers to join other teams. Later that year, he signed with E. B. Lamar's

Cuban X-Giants from Philadelphia. Foster lost the first game he pitched for his new team but won his next forty-four starts and finished the regular season with a record of fifty-four wins and one loss.[7] At the end of the 1903 season, the X-Giants faced Sol White's Philadelphia Giants in a series billed as the "Colored Championship of the World." In the eight-game series, Foster himself accounted for four wins, helping the X-Giants win the series five games to two.[8]

In 1904, Foster left the X-Giants and joined White's Philadelphia Giants for more money. Foster led the team to three championships over a three-year period. As a pitcher, he dominated African American baseball during the early 1900s. In 1905, by his own account, he won fifty-one of fifty-five games against black major and minor league teams.[9]

Sol White added to the Rube Foster pitching mystique and influence by asking the Texan to write an article entitled "How to Pitch" for White's book on African American baseball, *Sol White's Official Base Ball Guide*. The book, first published in 1907, was one of the first histories of African American baseball. White recounted the history of recent important Negro League games, documented how black baseball was played, and offered tutorials on how to pitch and hit in order to assist younger players.

Foster's contribution fell into the tutorial category. He described his theories on pitching and the pitcher's importance to the game. He stated that "it matters not how strong the infield or outfield may be, or how fast a team is on the bases, the strength of all base ball nines lies in their pitchers."[10] Foster went on to stress the importance of conditioning and stretching. "Conditioning," he said, "is the main essential to pitching."[11] He also advised pitchers to never fully "let out," meaning not throw the ball as hard as they could, until their arms became loose.[12]

Foster's advice, revolutionary at the time, became common practice at all levels of baseball by the end of the century. He told young pitchers to maintain a positive attitude, because no matter how well he pitches, every pitcher becomes wild at times. While most pitchers compensated for a lack of control by lessening their speed and throwing the ball straight over the plate, Foster recommended using a curve ball when in trouble. The curve had the potential of fooling the batter. He also stressed that a pitcher should be able to field his position.[13]

Foster ended his article with his three principles for good pitching: "good control, when to pitch certain balls, and where to pitch them."[14] He stressed that the longer a pitcher played the game, the better he became through experience. Through this experience, pitchers would achieve victories. Foster concluded his article with the advice, "If at first you don't succeed, try again."[15] Foster received national publicity from his writing. African American fans that never saw him pitch learned of his ability and perceived him as the greatest black pitcher.

Foster's connection to Texas, and his importance to the black community, increased as his accomplishments received more notice in the black press. While no white major league pitcher, manager, or team ever admitted to reading or using Foster's ideas, Foster himself claimed that more than one team secretly invited him to their spring training camps to coach their pitchers. Two teams that Foster claimed to have helped were Connie Mack's Philadelphia Athletics and John McGraw's New York Giants. Foster said that his advice led the Giants' great pitcher Christy Mathewson to develop skills that eventually led to Mathewson's induction into the National Baseball Hall of Fame.[16]

Writing for White's book was an immense honor and increased Foster's reputation as a knowledgeable and dominant pitcher in black baseball. Then in 1907, he left the Philadelphia Giants following a contract dispute with White. Foster returned to Chicago to play for Frank Leland and his team, which at that time went by the name Leland Giants.[17] Foster's return marked a turning point in his career. Until 1907, his influence on baseball and the African American community went no further than his reputation as a star pitcher. Beginning in 1907 with the Leland Giants, Foster sought a greater role in African American baseball. This started with the contract he signed with Leland. Besides pitching for Leland's team, Foster also received complete control over bookings.[18]

Just the presence of Rube Foster on the Leland Giants' roster drew fans to games. Foster was the most popular and dominant player in African American baseball. Since Foster could not pitch every game, though, Leland named him team manager in order to increase attendance. The idea was that given Foster's reputation for strategy, black fans would expect something exciting and extraordinary from him as manager.

Foster accepted the position wholeheartedly. He proceeded to rebuild the Giants based on his own ideas. He signed away star players from other teams, such as the Cuban X-Giants' future Hall of Fame shortstop John Henry Lloyd. Using his new players, Foster created a team centered on speed. The offensive strategy of the Leland Giants focused almost entirely on the use of the hit-and-run. Every player ran while on the base paths, and the squad attempted to steal on almost every pitch. The players also attempted to get an extra base with each hit. This constant motion wore greatly on the nerves of opposing pitchers. Pitchers who worried too much about the base runners tended to serve up more good pitches to the batters, thus improving the Giants' chances of getting hits. At the same time, if the pitcher ignored the base runner to focus attention on getting out the batter, the players stole bases, easily moving men into scoring position.[19]

One invention by Foster, the bunt-and-run, exemplified his philosophy of speed and constant motion on the base paths. With fast players on first base and at bat, the runner broke for second on the pitch, as if to steal the base. The batter then bunted the ball down the third-base line. The runner on base continued to run, rounded second, and ended up at third. If the third baseman for the opposition came in to field the bunt, leaving third base unprotected, the base runner took third easily. If the third baseman stayed back and covered his base, the pitcher or catcher had to field the ball, giving both runners time to reach base safely.[20]

Foster's impact on the Leland Giants and Negro League baseball extended beyond his role as a player and manager to his control of the team's finances. Foster's negotiations set the model for how future black organizations would operate. At the time he took over booking, the Giants made around one hundred fifty dollars a game. Foster negotiated new contracts with the owners of the stadiums at which the team played that gave the Giants 40 percent of the gate receipts. The percentage later rose to 50. These percentages were considerably higher than for any other African American team. As a result, the Giants began making more than five hundred dollars a game.[21]

The financial maneuvering by Foster paralleled changes in African American society at the time. Excluded from white society, African Americans developed their own businesses. As these businesses became more profitable during the twentieth century, black business owners increased their bargaining power in dealings with other African Americans, and even with whites.

The contracts negotiated by Foster proved important since the Leland Giants played all of their games at stadiums owned by white businessmen, who usually received the majority of the profits from games and did not particularly enjoy sharing their money with anyone. Playing in the Chicago

City League, the Leland Giants scheduled games on Saturdays and Sundays before white major league games. Foster's demands for an equal portion of the gate seem even more ambitious considering that these white owners, such as Charles Comiskey of the Chicago White Sox, were legendary for making the largest possible profit off their teams and their stinginess concerning players' salaries. Still, the owners agreed to Foster's terms.

Foster was professionally ambitious and pursued even more control over the Leland Giants. He saw himself as the proprietor of African American baseball. He believed only he knew the best way to run black baseball and that only he had the ability to make decisions that governed its future.[22] With his goals firmly in mind, Foster moved to take complete control of the Leland Giants in 1909. He demanded that owner Frank Leland remove himself from all aspects of operations and hand over complete financial and managerial control. Leland would remain team owner, but in name only.[23] Leland, of course, refused, and the two men began a yearlong battle for the team.

A decisive moment in the power struggle occurred in mid-July when Foster suffered an injury in a game against the Cuban Stars. He left the game in the first inning, walking off the mound without any help. Later the team doctor discovered a small broken bone in his foot.[24] The injury kept Foster out of the lineup for six weeks, during which time he missed a series against the St. Paul Colored Gophers. The Giants lost the series, costing Leland's team the title of "Colored Champions of the World."[25]

Questions soon arose about whether Foster faked his injury in order to hurt Leland during their struggle for control. No concrete evidence exists regarding the severity of the injury or its impact on Foster's health. What is known is that Foster would go to almost any length to achieve his goals. His players claimed that he froze baseballs the day before games to deaden them and banked the baseline on his home field to help his team's bunts stay fair.[26] While this evidence is circumstantial, when the Leland Giants played the Chicago Cubs of the National League in a three-game exhibition series in October of 1909, Foster made a miraculous recovery. The opportunity to prove himself, and to a lesser extent defend the ability of his race, was too great. Foster declared himself fit to pitch the last game of the series. Unfortunately, the Cubs swept the series.[27]

In October, Foster gave Leland one final demand: turn over complete control of the team, or Foster would leave and create his own squad. Leland refused and Foster quit. Before he made this ultimatum, though, Foster had already laid the foundation to proceed on his own. He acquired aid from two of Leland's financial backers, Major R. R. Jackson and Beauregard Moseley. Foster also took with him the majority of the Leland Giants' star players, including John Henry Lloyd and Grant "Home Run" Johnson. Foster also named his new team the Leland Giants for the name recognition.[28]

Leland responded to Foster's actions by filing suit to keep him from using the name Leland Giants. Foster and his financial backers countersued, claiming he had the right to the team name, despite the fact that the team was named after Leland.[29] When the lawsuits finally reached court, Foster won the rights to the name. Frank Leland, though, received the lease to Auburn Park, the stadium in Chicago where the original Leland Giants played.[30]

The reasoning behind the judge's decision remained a mystery. With the decision, though, Foster acquired his own team with a name the public knew. With his move to govern all of African American baseball under way, Foster refused to let a minor inconvenience like lack of a stadium hinder his dreams. He obtained, with the help of his chief financial backer, Beauregard Moseley, and John Schorling, a white Chicago businessman, Old Roman's ballpark in Chicago, previously owned by Charles Comiskey and used by the White Sox. Old Roman's was located just half a mile from Auburn Park, which allowed Foster to compete directly with Frank Leland and the new Chicago Giants.[31] After signing away players from other black teams throughout the country, Foster fielded an all-star team of Negro League greats. His new team drew crowds large enough to put Leland out of business, thus making Foster the dominant figure for African American baseball in the Windy City.[32] With Frank Leland and Chicago conquered, Foster moved to control all of black baseball.

At the same time, Foster maintained ties with his home state. In April of 1910, he took his Leland Giants on a preseason tour of Texas. In Fort Worth, more than three thousand people turned out to watch the team. Led by Texas pitcher "Smokey" Joe Williams, the Giants defeated the local club, the Black Wonders.[33] The Leland Giants also beat the Houston Black Buffaloes, Dallas Black Giants, and Prairie View College Panthers during the tour.[34] This marked the second straight year the Leland Giants toured Texas. During the 1909 season, the *Indianapolis Freeman* reported that when the Giants arrived in Fort Worth, fans gave Foster "a welcome that would have done honor to the President of the United States."[35] Similar receptions occurred throughout the state, wherever the Giants played. The *Indianapolis Freeman* went on to state, "The ovation from men of every walk of life given Foster gives prominence to the high esteem of the people all over the country."[36] For the remainder of his career, Foster continued these spring training games in his home state, allowing him to advance black baseball in Texas. And these games united Lone Star blacks with black communities throughout the country.

Furthermore, by maintaining his ties to Texas, Foster enhanced the reputation of the state as a hotbed of baseball talent. When reporters for the major black newspapers in places like Chicago and Indianapolis wrote about Foster, they often referred to him as the "big Texan" and commented on the level of talent that existed in his native state. As a result, as Foster worked to dominate black baseball in America, black baseball in Texas earned national recognition, and black Texans had another point of reference to defend their masculinity.

Foster sought to extend his control over African American baseball by removing several of his competitors. In 1910, he warned other African American baseball owners of a trouble that Foster claimed threatened all black baseball. The trouble, according to Foster, involved white owners of black baseball teams. Foster told the other black owners they must remove all forms of racial impurity from their sport for black baseball to survive.[37] On the surface, his message appeared to be a call for African Americans to take control of their lives. The charge for black ownership fit into the black nationalism movement in the United States. At the same time, though, the goal of removing all white influences fit Foster's plan for controlling all of African American baseball. The white owners and businessmen he wanted out of black baseball were some of the most powerful men in the sport. Removing these men created a power void that Foster planned to fill. His main target became Nat Strong of New York, the dominant white booking agent on the East Coast.

Foster carried out a simple plan; he took his team, which he renamed the Chicago American Giants, on a barnstorming tour of the East Coast. The American Giants played several exhibition games in New York and Philadelphia, allowing Foster's team to develop a large fan base in the East. Foster also paid his players more than Strong did, $150 a month to Strong's $75.[38] The higher salaries allowed Foster to sign away many of Strong's best players and thus attract the baseball fans in New York. Much to Foster's chagrin, he never succeeded in driving Strong out of black baseball, but his efforts did decrease Strong's prominence. Foster became the dominant power in African American baseball in both Chicago and New York.

While Foster and Strong battled for supremacy in Chicago and New York, other black entrepreneurs appeared in the world of baseball. Teams such as the Topeka Giants, run by "Topeka" Jack Johnson, and the Kansas City Giants, run by Tobe Smith, existed outside the control of the dominant figures in African American baseball. The teams played in the western states and tapped into a relatively ignored large and loyal fan base during the 1910s. The popularity of black baseball in the West caused eastern teams to take notice and regularly schedule series against the western teams. Foster's was one of the first eastern black baseball teams to face western teams. (The American Giants, part of the African American baseball establishment, competed primarily against eastern teams and was thus seen as an eastern team.) In 1910, three thousand fans turned out for one game in St. Louis to watch Foster's Chicago American Giants play the St. Louis Giants.[39]

Foster, eyeing the situation in the West, gave thought to starting his own black league in 1910. He wrote: "In my opinion, the time is now at hand when the formation of colored leagues should receive much consideration. In fact, I believe it is absolutely necessary."[40] To accomplish his goal, Foster sent his financial backer, Beauregard Moseley, to find other teams willing to join the prospective league. Mosley stressed to potential league members that since the white leagues barred blacks from competing, African Americans must form their own leagues to achieve legitimacy in the sport. This argument resonated with the audiences and fit into the larger movement around the country of establishing black-owned businesses as a counter to segregation. As a result, Moseley received commitments from several teams to join the new league, including franchises in St. Louis, Kansas City, Mobile, and Louisville. Unfortunately, Foster's all-black baseball league never received proper funding from team owners and sponsors within the different cities. Without the proper backing, the league and teams found it impossible to meet the expected expenses of the season, such as equipment and umpires. As a result, the teams in the western towns chose to play as independent barnstormers, a status that required less overhead. The league failed before it even began.[41] Foster kept his plan for an African American league in the back of his mind and made sure to schedule games every year for the Chicago American Giants throughout the South and West.

A new threat to Foster's dream of dominating black baseball soon appeared in the form of Charles I. Taylor. Born in South Carolina in 1872, Taylor became the co-owner and manager of the Indianapolis ABCs in 1914. Borrowing a page from Foster's own managerial book, Taylor signed star players away from other western teams. Taylor also stood up to Foster, refusing to give him 50 percent of the gate for a possible Chicago American Giants and Indianapolis ABCs game.[42]

This challenge to his authority greatly angered Foster. When Taylor refused to agree to the terms set by Foster, Foster verbally attacked Taylor. In the *Indianapolis Freeman*, a leading African American newspaper in the country, Foster called Taylor an ingrate. He stated that in the past Taylor came to him for advice on players, and that he, Foster, more than once paid train fare for eastern baseball teams to come west and play Taylor's ABCs.[43] Foster believed that these actions proved his predominance over Taylor and the rest of black baseball, and therefore Taylor needed to defer to Foster's judgment. The fact that Taylor stood up to him caused Foster to feel publicly slighted.

The animosity between the two men flowed both ways, though. While Taylor regarded Foster as a great baseball mind, he said Foster's intentions appeared to be to destroy his opponents through false accusations and misrepresentation.[44] Taylor also used the *Indianapolis Freeman* as a forum to promote himself and his team and to challenge Foster. In the paper, Taylor claimed he and other promoters played as much of a role in the success of black baseball as did Foster.[45]

In 1915, Foster and Taylor put aside their differences and decided to face each other on the playing field. The two men signed a contract for the Indianapolis ABCs to play the Chicago American Giants in a series of games in Indianapolis. The men agreed to split the profits from the series fifty-fifty. Despite the mutual agreement, no love was lost between the two. Exemplifying their animosity, the two team managers posed for pictures before the series began, but refused to stand next to each other. The editors of the black newspaper in Indianapolis provided a buffer between Foster and Taylor in all of the group pictures.[46]

The series between the two teams turned into complete pandemonium. A strong windstorm blew throughout the first game on July 18. The American Giants led the ABCs by a score of 3 to 2 going into the bottom of the eighth inning. The ABCs came to bat and quickly got a single and three consecutive walks, forcing in the tying run.[47] With the score tied and the bases loaded with no outs, Foster asked that the game be stopped, arguing that dirt blown around the infield by the windstorm was getting in his players' eyes and blinding them. Foster then demanded the umpire make the ABCs halt the game and wet down the infield to stop the blowing dirt. While Indianapolis watered down the infield, rain began to fall. The change in weather prompted Foster to then petition the umpire to call the game. If the umpire ended the game, the official score would revert back to where it stood at the end of the last full inning of play, 2 to 2, making the game a tie.[48]

Since the rainfall was not particularly heavy, the umpire ordered the contest to continue. As Foster continued to argue his case, the umpire became angry and forfeited the game to Indianapolis. Pete Hill, the American Giants captain, ran up to find out the umpire's decision. As he ran toward the umpire, the ABCs' players and fans rioted, rushing onto the field. Fortunately, no one suffered any injuries, but one police officer pulled his gun on an American Giants player.[49]

The next day, when the two teams met again, there were more incidents. In the bottom of the third inning, with the American Giants leading 2 to 0, a police sergeant came onto the playing field and accosted Foster. The sergeant berated Foster about the previous day's riot, calling him what Foster later described as the "dirtiest names I have ever had said to me."[50]

While the police sergeant verbally attacked Foster, Harry Bauchman, the American Giants third-base coach, experienced his own problems. Upon reaching the coach's box, Bauchman found the base out of line and used his foot to push the base back to its proper position. C. I. Taylor saw Bauchman touch the base, rushed from the bench, and accused Bauchman of trying to cheat by interfering with the playing field. Taylor then called the police from the stands. At that point, the police officers began, for reasons that remain unknown, beating Bauchman. The Chicago American Giants immediately forfeited the game and left the city of Indianapolis without playing the third game.[51]

Foster explained the events in a letter to the *Indianapolis Freeman*. He used the incident to attack Taylor. Foster claimed in both incidents that he never lost his temper, questioned the judgment of an umpire, or talked back to the police. He said the players on both teams and the fans deserved no blame for the incident. All blame fell upon ABCs' owner Thomas Bowser and manager C. I. Taylor. These men, whom Foster called "low down and dirty," ordered the police onto the field, according to Foster, and were destroying the integrity of African American baseball.[52]

Taylor defended himself, writing his own letter to the *Freeman*. Taylor called Foster's accusations false, even libelous. Furthermore, Taylor stated, no player except for Bauchman was ever physically attacked, and Bauchman provoked his attack by "spiking and stabbing" the base with his shoes.[53] Taylor apologized for the physical assault on Bauchman and the verbal assault on Foster, but also stated that he never ordered any of the attacks. He concluded by calling Foster's charges strictly a means of covering up for the fact that the ABCs swept the American Giants.[54]

Foster decided in 1917 to renew his goal of creating a professional African American league. He invited the owners of the significant black baseball teams from throughout the Midwest, including C. I. Taylor of the Indianapolis ABCs, to Indianapolis to discuss plans for the upcoming baseball season.[55] When the other owners arrived, Foster spoke of his life in baseball. He traced his career as a pitcher, manager, and owner. He also discussed the inequalities between teams in black baseball and revealed his plan to create a professional African American league.[56] Foster hoped that his reputation as a dominant player, owner, and manager would convince the other owners to agree that a professional black baseball league was needed. Unfortunately, he did not convince, and the league failed to materialize yet again.

Foster refused to give up, and in April his dream received some help from an unlikely source, the U.S. government. That month the United States entered World War I. The government's need for manpower in factories and defense industries to assist with the war effort prompted a massive migration of African Americans from the South to northern cities. In roughly three years, close to five hundred thousand African Americans moved north.[57] Settling in all-black neighborhoods, these African Americans provided the future fan base that made a black baseball league possible. Black-owned baseball teams came to play a major role in the development of a larger African American culture. Combined with other black-owned businesses, Foster's eventual league served as a source of pride and identity for a national black community.

In 1917, Foster worked to take advantage of the number of people moving to the larger American cities. In Chicago, he held a Texas Day celebration, appealing to the black immigrants from his home state. As the central feature of the celebration, the American Giants faced a traveling team known as the Texas Stars. To add to the pageantry of the game, Colonel Franklin Dennison of the U.S. Army and Illinois state representative Major Robert Jackson, both of whom were white, threw out the first pitches. The Texas Stars were a semiprofessional team; so to keep the contest competitive, Foster started a pitcher by the name of Whitworth who had sat out the majority of the 1917 season with an injury. This move also allowed Foster not to waste any of his stars against an inferior team. Even with an injured pitcher, the American Giants won easily, thrilling the thousands of fans who turned out. The contest allowed the former southerners to connect with their new community while preserving their old identity.[58]

Foster's dreams were put on hold, though, as he and the other black baseball owners around the country saw many of their players leave to fight in the war. Star players such as John Henry Lloyd and "Bullet Joe" Rogan left their teams to serve in Europe. Seven players from the ABCs were drafted, including the team's star, Dave Malarcher.[59] Foster's team lost eight players to the armed forces.[60]

Foster hoped that after the war he could create his league, but in 1919 his dream experienced another setback as Chicago erupted in a race riot. Foster and the American Giants returned from a road trip to find the National Guard using their stadium as a camp. As a result, the club canceled all its home games for more than a month.[61]

Looking over the situation confronting black baseball, Foster decided the sport needed to reform itself in order to survive the war and gain credibility among the nation's public. The problem, as Foster saw it, centered on the nonprofessionalism of the black teams. The stealing of players from each other, along with the personal arguments and grudges between the owners, kept black baseball teams from proving wrong any white accusations of low-caliber and bush-league baseball.[62] Following World War I, Foster's ideas were well received by other owners, managers, and newspapermen associated with African American baseball. The irony of Foster's call for reform was that he personally was guilty of the problems he claimed were holding back black baseball.

On February 13 and 14, 1920, Foster met in Kansas City with several owners of black baseball teams about the creation of his league, which he called the Western Circuit of the Negro National Baseball League, or the Negro National League (NNL) for short. Under the new league's constitution, Foster became the president. Every team in the circuit agreed to play when, where, and against whomever Foster ordered. All the teams purchased their equipment from him. Foster defended these clauses, claiming the league saved more money by purchasing all of the equipment at one time.[63]

He also knew that every team had to be competitive for the league to draw fans and to survive. Therefore, to give all the teams an equal chance at winning, as well as to destroy rumors that he created the league to benefit the American Giants, Foster moved his, and other, star players around to different teams. He moved outfielder Oscar Charleston from the Chicago American Giants to the Indianapolis ABCs, pitchers Jose Mendez and Sam Crawford from Detroit to Kansas City, and many others until the teams appeared equal in talent.[64] On top of the player movements, Foster included a rule in the league's bylaws preventing players from jumping teams or teams from raiding each other for players. To help protect the owners financially, he created a pool of league dues. This money would be used to assist teams that fell on hard times, thus allowing them to pay their expenses and continue to compete.[65]

Foster dominated every aspect of the new league's business. The creation of the Negro National League marked the culmination of his lifelong dream of controlling black baseball. He ran the entire league, receiving 10 percent of the gate from every game as payment.[66] The league proved so popular that it overshadowed African American baseball throughout the rest of the nation. The NNL received the majority of its coverage in black newspapers throughout the country and became the largest black-owned industry in America. Foster achieved his kingdom; his only remaining challenge was to maintain his position atop the sport.

Foster and the league still faced many problems. First of all, though the Indianapolis ABCs and the Chicago American Giants played the first league game on May 2, 1920, most of the teams in the league were not ready to play until July.[67] Many of the squads lacked ballparks. Only three teams, Chicago, Detroit, and St. Louis, maintained access to permanent playing facilities. The other teams in the league played games only when an open date existed at the local white parks. As a result, the teams played unequal numbers of games, scuttling Foster's original plan for each team to play a one-hundred-game schedule. One team, the Cuban Stars, had no stadium and as a result played their entire first season as a traveling road team. The Stars finally received access to a stadium in Cincinnati in 1921.[68]

Foster single-handedly made his league survive. If a team ran out of money while on the road, he wired them enough to get home. If a team appeared to be on the edge of bankruptcy, he kept them alive by forwarding pay.[69] He also continued to shift players to keep weak clubs competitive. One clause in the league's charter required home teams to guarantee 35 percent of the profits from the gate to the visiting team.[70] Unfortunately, 35 percent amounted to nothing if only a small number of fans attended. To compensate the teams, Foster supplemented the gate with his own money.[71] His league also furthered black baseball in Texas, with the majority of league's teams, such as the Kansas City Monarchs and Indianapolis ABCs, joining the Chicago American Giants for spring training in Texas. By having the teams train in his home state, Foster ensured that the local African American community gained a connection and sense of unity with African American communities throughout the country.

Foster's efforts to keep the league going dominated his time. As a result, he cut back on his duties with the American Giants. In 1922, he turned over his position as team manager to his third baseman, Dave Malarcher.[72] The loss of control proved difficult for Foster, since he had worked so hard to establish his team, but the move was a sacrifice for the larger goal of league success. Unfortunately, Foster's obsession with the Negro National League cost him more than the Chicago American Giants.

From 1920 to 1926, Foster gave everything he had to keep the league running. He survived the creation of a new league, the Eastern Colored League, by Ed Bolden and Nat Strong in 1921. Foster saw his league lose many of its stars to the new circuit. Bolden and Strong followed the example set by Foster and paid higher salaries in order to steal players away from the NNL. To deal with the problem, Foster reached an agreement with Bolden and Strong that neither league would sign away the other's players. Furthermore, the two leagues agreed their champions would meet each year in the Negro World Series to crown the undisputed champion of African American baseball. This move followed the model established by the white American League and National League in 1903.

Despite its success as the largest black-owned business in the country, the NNL still experienced hardships. In 1923, the league lost four teams, Toledo, Milwaukee, Pittsburgh, and Cleveland. Then in 1924, the Indianapolis ABCs folded when their owner and manager at the time, C. I. Taylor, died. Without Taylor's leadership, the ABCs found it impossible to exist, a fate experienced by numerous African American baseball teams and businesses during the late 1920s and 1930s. NNL gate receipts declined. While all the teams made a profit in 1921, by 1924 every team lost money. Foster, though, fought tooth and nail to save the league. He used money from the Chicago American Giants, the most profitable team in the league, to bail out teams on the verge of bankruptcy.[73]

In May of 1925, Foster suffered a major physical setback. He went to Indianapolis to try to restart the ABCs. That night, a gas pipe in his hotel room burst, almost killing him. He survived only because a stranger smelled the fumes and dragged Foster to safety. The accident severely reduced Foster's lung capacity, making him more susceptible to illness.[74] Furthermore, the exposure to the gas and lack of oxygen to his brain possibly contributed to his mental illness later in life.

By 1926, all the years of mental stress had caught up with Foster. Rumors circulated throughout the black press and baseball community of his erratic behavior. Pitcher Willie Powell, who played for the Chicago American Giants, claimed he saw Foster chasing imaginary fly balls in the street outside his home.[75] Foster also ran over a woman with his car, an accident for which he gave no explanation or defense. On another occasion, Foster locked himself in his office bathroom and refused to come out for several hours. In the summer of 1926, Foster's wife called the Chicago police to restrain him when he suddenly began smashing the furniture in the family home without provocation. Later in the summer, the police arrested Foster when he attacked a friend with an ice pick. When the attack case went to trial, the judge ruled Foster was mentally insane and committed him to Kankakee Asylum in Illinois, where he lived the rest of his life.[76]

The Negro National League tried to continue without Foster. In 1927, the league owners elected a new commissioner, G. B. Key, Foster's vice president, and sold the Chicago American Giants to a new owner.[77] Attendance rapidly decreased. Teams changed hands and dropped out of the league. In 1930, at the age of forty-two, Andrew "Rube" Foster died in the Kankakee Asylum. Shortly after his death, the Negro National League disbanded.

With the death of Foster, African American baseball lost the most influential person ever involved with the game. Despite his faults, he changed the way the country perceived African American baseball and black players. First as an ace pitcher from Texas, and later as a manager, owner, and commissioner of the Negro National League, Foster elevated black baseball from the bush leagues to major league and professional status.

Foster's accomplishments also proved important for African American baseball in Texas. By establishing himself as the most important person in the sport, Foster furthered Texas's reputation as a top location for talent. Foster's name became synonymous among African Americans with the state. Foster became linked with every black baseball player to come out of Texas in the first half of the 1900s. When African American newspapers discussed Negro League players from Texas, such as Willie Wells, the papers noted that the Texas-born player hailed from the same state as Rube Foster.

Furthermore, Foster and his league played a major role in the development of a national African American community and culture. The success of his team and league coincided with movements in the country to establish black-owned institutions to challenge racial segregation. Foster's success as a pitcher, and the accomplishments of the players he managed, presented favorable images of black masculinity and refuted the scientific racism prevalent in the United States at the time. Finally, the growth of his league was one consequence of the Great Migration to large northern cities during the World War I era and the 1920s. Baseball helped unify the new arrivals.

Fifty years after his death, Foster's legacy and impact on the game of baseball were recognized when, in 1981, he was inducted into the National Baseball Hall of Fame in Cooperstown, New York.

William "Willie" Foster, the top left-handed pitcher in Negro League history.
National Baseball Hall of Fame Library, Cooperstown, N.Y.

Smokey Joe, Biz, and the Devil
BLACK TEXANS WHO SHAPED THE GAME

4 Other Texans built on the legacy of Rube Foster and helped shape the Negro leagues and the game of baseball. These players also further promoted images of black masculinity through their reputations for physical and intellectual dominance in the game, and helped define the African American community in Texas and the nation. From Texas came players such as pitcher Willie Foster, Rube's half brother, catcher Louis Santop, pitcher Hilton Smith, and pitcher Andy Cooper. All four men are members of the National Baseball Hall of Fame. Willie Foster became the dominant left-handed pitcher in black baseball during the 1920s and 1930s. Known as the "Black Cy Young," he won more games than any other Negro League pitcher.

Santop, a native of Tyler, became the first great African American home-run hitter. One legend has it that Santop, as a member of the New York Lincoln Giants, could hit a sign in the Newark, New Jersey, stadium with a batted ball, 443 feet from home plate. A local tailor had promised to give any player who hit the sign a free suit. Santop won three new suits in one game.[1]

Santop played from 1909 to 1926. He began his career playing for the Fort Worth Wonders and later played for teams in Austin and San Antonio. On these early Texas teams, Santop played against fellow future Negro

Louis Santop, one of the great power hitters in the Negro leagues.
National Baseball Hall of Fame Library, Cooperstown, N.Y.

Hilton Smith, top pitcher who won twenty games or more annually over a twelve-year period with the Kansas City Monarchs. National Baseball Hall of Fame Library, Coopers-town, N.Y.

League star "Smokey" Joe Williams. In the Negro leagues, Santop went on to serve as the battery mate of Williams and of other great African American pitchers like "Cannonball" Dick Redding and Rube Foster. Santop posted a .316 lifetime batting average and even batted .324 in Negro League games at the end of his career.[2] As a member of the Philadelphia Hilldales club, Santop played in the first Colored World Series in 1924.[3]

Hilton Smith was born in Giddings, Texas, in 1907. He began his career with the Austin Black Senators, before playing twelve years for the Kansas City Monarchs of the Negro National League. Smith won twenty or more games in each of his twelve years, including a record of twenty-five wins and one loss in 1941.[4] Smith's biggest claim to fame, though, came as Satchel Paige's relief pitcher. To increase attendance, Paige started most games but pitched only the first couple of innings. Smith, who also played first base, then relieved Paige and pitched the final six or seven innings.[5] Smith was inducted into the Baseball Hall of Fame in 2001.

Andy Cooper, pitching star for the Detroit Stars and Kansas City Monarchs during the 1920s and 1930s. National Baseball Hall of Fame Library, Cooperstown, N.Y.

Born in Waco in 1896, Andy Cooper also achieved induction into the Hall of Fame. Recognized as the second-best left-handed pitcher in Negro League history, behind Willie Foster, Cooper served as the ace of the Kansas City Monarchs and Detroit Stars during the 1920s and 1930s. His control, impressive array of pitches including breaking pitches, and intelligence on the mound made him one of the most respected and successful pitchers of his era.[6]

Another Texan, Newt Allen, established himself as the dominant second baseman in the Negro leagues. During the 1930s, Allen and shortstop Willie Wells formed an all-Texan, all-star middle infield combination, first with the Kansas City Monarchs and later for the Homestead Grays. Former Negro leaguer Bill Drake recalled Allen's ability at second base, saying, "He wouldn't even look at first base on the pivot. He'd throw the ball to first under his left arm."[7]

The success of these players, and others, served as rallying points for the Texas black community. Just the nicknames given to the players brought to mind powerful images and reinforced black masculinity. For example, Louis Santop was called "Big Bertha" after the famous World War I cannon because of his monumental home runs.

Three other natives had an even greater influence on African American baseball, images of black masculinity, and the development of an African American community and culture. These three, "Smokey" Joe Williams, Willie "El Diablo" Wells, and Raleigh "Biz" Mackey, shaped black baseball more than anyone from Texas except Rube Foster. Included in every all-time greatest team for African American baseball, these men became synonymous with their positions and came to define how the game was to be played. And as with Rube Foster, the accomplishments of these players brought recognition and credibility to African American baseball in Texas.

"Smokey" Joe Williams, so nicknamed for his blinding fastball, pitched for more than thirty years, establishing himself as the greatest pitcher in Negro League history. In 1952, the *Pittsburgh Courier* asked a group of circuit veterans and African American sportswriters, including John Henry Lloyd, James "Cool Papa" Bell, and Oscar Charleston, to select an all-time "dream team." For the position of pitcher, the selection committee chose Williams over other greats such as Satchel Paige and Rube Foster.[8]

Gifted with amazing speed, Williams presented an ominous physical presence on the mound. Half Native American with strong facial features, Williams stood six feet, six inches tall. He was lanky in stature and pitched with a relaxed, overhand motion. Williams's long arms created such velocity when he pitched that the baseball seemed to explode when it hit the catcher's mitt. Some Negro leaguers who played with Williams claimed his fastball was so powerful that it could pass through a wall.[9]

Williams's success against the best pitchers from around the country, both black and white, gave African Americans in Texas a focus for racial pride. In arguing Williams's superiority to Walter Johnson or Christy Mathewson, for example, black Texans were arguing their own superiority to the white society that imposed segregation upon them.

Sam Streeter, a pitcher on the Homestead Grays of Pittsburgh in the early 1930s with Williams, recalled Williams's power: "If I was going to pick a man to throw hard, I'd have to pick Joe Williams. . . . It used to take two catchers to hold him. By the time the fifth inning was over, that catcher's

"Smokey" Joe Williams, a dominating power pitcher whom many in black baseball considered the best pitcher ever. National Baseball Hall of Fame Library, Cooperstown, N.Y.

hand would be all swollen. He'd have to have another catcher there the rest of the game."[10] From 1912 to 1932, Williams ranked as the best pitcher in professional African American baseball. During this period, besides beating the best black teams of the day, he also faced the best white pitchers in exhibition games. In these games, Williams compiled a record of twenty-two wins, seven losses, and one tie. Of his seven losses, two occurred after he reached the age of forty-five. Williams also amassed a record of eight wins, two losses, and one tie against both black and white pitchers later inducted into the National Baseball Hall of Fame. Among this list of opponents, he defeated such white stars as Grover Cleveland Alexander and Walter Johnson.[11] Bill Yancey, a former teammate, said, "With 'Smokey' Joe Williams . . . pitching we could beat anybody."[12]

The white newspapers around the country generally refused to print any stories covering these exhibition games, especially if the African American team won. However, the national black press celebrated these contests. When Joe Williams defeated Walter Johnson, for example, African Americans framed these interracial games as the best pitcher in African American baseball competing equally with, and emerging victorious against, the best pitcher in white baseball.[13] Like Jack Johnson, the black heavyweight boxer from Galveston who was champion in the early 1900s, Williams served as a powerful example of black masculinity.

Born in the town of Seguin, Texas, Williams left the actual date of his birth a mystery. In an interview with the *Chicago Defender*, he claimed his birth year as 1876.[14] Other accounts placed it as early as 1874. The Seguin Baptist Church records showed the baptism of a baby named Joe Williams in 1885, while his marriage license listed April 1, 1886, as his date of birth.[15] Whatever his birth year, Williams pitched until 1932, an impressive feat considering he was between forty-six and fifty-eight years old when he retired.

Fans and historians have wondered how Williams learned to pitch and when he began his career. Williams once answered the question by saying, "Someone gave me a ball at an early age, and it was my companion for a long time. . . . I carried it in my pocket and slept with it under my pillow. I always wanted to pitch."[16] His career began with several semiprofessional teams in the San Antonio area, where he won twenty-eight games and lost only four in 1905. Unfortunately, not much is known of his time with these squads except for his overall record. Even the names of the teams have been lost.

In 1906, Williams moved to the Austin area, winning fifteen games and losing nine for other semiprofessional teams. In 1907, he returned to San Antonio, joining the semiprofessional San Antonio Black Bronchos. Williams pitched for the Bronchos for the next three years. During this stint, he posted an impressive win-loss record, going twenty and eight in 1907 and twenty and two in 1908. The following year, he began the season with the Black Bronchos but left the team midway through to join the professional Birmingham Black Barons from Alabama. Williams won a combined total of thirty-two games to only eight losses for the two teams that year.[17]

Following the end of the season, Williams returned to San Antonio. His reputation as a dominant pitcher had spread outside of Texas. Fans and players heard stories about how in one game for San Antonio in 1909, Williams struck out fourteen batters and gave up only one hit in a 5 to 0 victory over the New Orleans Black Eagles.[18]

In 1910, Frank Leland's Leland Giants, managed by Rube Foster, came to San Antonio as a part of a preseason barnstorming tour. Williams beat Foster's team, the best team in African American baseball at the time, 3 to 0. Foster teased Williams during the game, asking the pitcher to slow his pitches down to allow the Leland Giants to hit the ball. Williams responded, "Do you really want me to throw hard? If I really throw hard, they won't even see it at all."[19] Impressed by the ability and confidence of the youngster, Foster signed Williams on the spot to a contract with his team. Owner Frank Leland described his new pitcher's ability: "If you have ever witnessed a pebble in a storm you have not seen the equal of the speed possessed by this wonderful Texas giant. He is the king of all pitchers hailing from the Lone Star state and you have but to see him once to exclaim, 'That's a-plenty.'"[20] Leland's hyperbole may be related to his fight with Foster for control of the team. By declaring Williams the greatest pitcher ever from Texas, Leland lessened Foster's importance.

Shortly after joining the Leland Giants, Williams left the team to join their crosstown rivals, the Chicago Giants, presumably for more money. Playing in Chicago for the Giants offered Williams national exposure, especially considering that the *Chicago Defender* was one of the country's leading African American newspapers. The national black press spread stories of Williams's accomplishments on the diamond. In one game against the Fisk Colts, a white minor league team, he won the game for himself. In addition to striking out eleven Colts and not giving up any runs, Williams hit a solo home run in the seventh inning. His home run proved the only run scored in the game.[21] A week later, he pitched both games of a double-header, winning the first game 6 to 0 and the second 9 to 2.[22]

In 1912, Williams left the Chicago Giants and joined the New York Lincoln Giants for a higher salary. The new team combined Williams with such great players as shortstop John Henry Lloyd, catcher and fellow Texan Louis Santop, and pitcher "Cannonball" Dick Redding, all of whom are in the National Baseball Hall of Fame. As a result, the New York Lincoln Giants became one of the premier teams in African American baseball, winning roughly nineteen out of every twenty games they played. Williams reached his prime as a pitcher during his ten years with the Lincoln Giants. Playing in New York City also gave Williams even more coverage in the major black newspapers throughout the country. His reputation as the best black pitcher allowed him to command a salary of one hundred and five dollars a month, while the rest of his teammates made between forty-five and seventy-five dollars.[23] Williams's exposure in New York also increased the reputation of black baseball in Texas. Other black pitchers from Texas began to be compared to Williams, and the black press and fans praised the state as a hotbed of baseball talent.

Williams was known not only for his speed but also his control and over-all pitching ability. Frank Forbes, an infielder for the Lincoln Giants, later recounted, "Joe had a lot of control. . . . He'd cut your throat up here with a fastball inside and then come down on the outside corner on your knees with the next one."[24] Judy Johnson, the Hall of Fame shortstop who managed Williams with the Homestead Grays, added, "If he walked one man, he'd say his control was bad."[25]

While playing with the Lincoln Giants, Williams began his impressive record against major leaguers. In 1912, he defeated the New York Giants, champions of the white National League, 6 to 0. In the game, Williams held the Giants to just four hits over nine innings. Two weeks later he beat the New York Highlanders of the white American League, later renamed the Yankees. Again he gave up only four hits and no runs, winning 6 to 0.[26]

In 1913, Williams faced white major league teams on five separate occasions, compiling a record of four victories and one loss. These games raised Williams's overall record against white professional teams to eight victories and one loss, a significant statistic for an African American pitcher at the time. That season the Lincoln Giants won a total of one hundred and one games with only six losses. This record made them one of the most formi-dable teams in baseball, black or white.[27]

The following year, Williams had possibly his best single season. He won an astounding forty-one games and lost only three.[28] He also contin-ued his dominance of white major league teams, not losing a game to any professional white team. In one game, Williams beat the National League champion Philadelphia Phillies 1 to 0. In the ninth inning, Williams struck out the side on nine straight pitches.[29] The same year he also threw a no-hitter against Portland, the champions of the white minor league Pacific Coast League.[30]

Williams faced Waite Hoyt, a future Hall of Fame pitcher, in 1916. Hoyt lead a team of white minor league all-stars against Williams and the Lincoln Giants. Williams proved too much for the white team, beating them 5 to 0.[31]

The year 1917 proved eventful for Williams. He defeated future Hall of Famers "Rube" Marquard of Brooklyn, 5 to 4, and "Chief" Bender of the Philadelphia Phillies, 11 to 1.[32] Then, pitching for one game with the Phila-delphia Hilldales, Williams turned in one of the best performances of his career. Against Christy Mathewson and the National League champion New York Giants, Williams threw a no-hitter and struck out twenty batters over ten innings. Unfortunately, he lost the game, 1 to 0, on an error in the bot-tom of the tenth.[33] Again, like Jack Johnson's defeat of Jim Jeffers in boxing, the victories by Williams, reported by black newspapers, reaffirmed black masculinity for thousands of African Americans throughout Texas and the country.

Williams was not always successful against white teams. While playing in Florida during the winter of 1915, Williams broke his pitching hand when he instinctively caught a line drive barehanded. After sitting out for several weeks, Williams returned to the mound, only to be hit again by another bat-ted ball, this time breaking his wrist. The injuries caused him to miss the majority of the season, but he returned to the pitching mound in the fall to again face the National League New York Giants. Still rusty from his period of inactivity, Williams gave up eleven hits and lost the game 4 to 2.[34]

But in another exhibition game against a white team the following week, Williams returned to form, pitching a 1–0 victory over the National League champion Philadelphia Phillies. In the game, Williams struck out ten bat-ters and allowed only five hits. He really showed the white players his amaz-ing talent in the fourth inning. The Phillies had loaded the bases with no outs. Williams then proceeded to strike out the next three batters. The *Philadelphia Bulletin* reported that "Joe's twister had the Phillies baffled."[35]

On opening day in 1919, he put on one of the most impressive performances in black baseball history. Williams faced his former teammate, "Cannonball" Dick Redding. The two men pitched both games of a doubleheader. Redding beat Williams in the first game by the score of 1 to 0. Williams came back to throw a no-hitter in the second game, winning 1 to 0.[36]

In 1924, at the age of at least thirty-eight, he left the Lincoln Giants and joined the Brooklyn Royal Giants, but he stayed with the team for only a season. The following year Cumberland Posey signed Williams to play for the Homestead Grays of Pittsburgh, one of the dominant teams in Negro League history. One account claims that in the seven years he pitched for the Grays, Williams lost only five games, while the team itself won one hundred and thirty games in 1925 and then lost only six the next season.[37]

With the Grays, an independent team not associated with either professional Negro league, Williams continued to mow down the hitters, white and black. In 1925, as the ace of the team's pitching staff, even at an age of at least thirty-nine, he started for the Grays in the decisive game of a three-game series against the Negro National League champion Kansas City Monarchs and won.[38] The next year Williams defeated an all-star team of white players from the American League, led by future Hall of Fame players Lefty Grove and Goose Goslin.[39] Then, in 1928, he threw the fifth no-hitter of his career in a game against a white semiprofessional team from Akron, Ohio. The same year, he beat Connie Mack's Philadelphia Athletics.[40]

In 1930, at the then reported age of forty-four, Williams showed he still possessed amazing pitching speed and ability. In one of the most famous accomplishments in black baseball history, Williams pitched a complete game shutout against the Kansas City Monarchs of the Negro National League. In the twelve-inning game, he struck out twenty-seven Monarchs and gave up only one hit.[41] Kansas City pitcher Chet Brewer, the loser in the game, remembered facing Williams that night, saying, "Joe could throw harder than anybody I batted against."[42]

The speed of Williams's fastball played an important role in another black baseball event. While pitching for the Homestead Grays in 1930, Williams threw his fastball so hard he split his catcher's finger open, making it impossible for the man to play. As Judy Johnson, the manager for the Grays, later recounted, the team possessed no backup catchers at the time; so they signed a local youth out of the stands to come and catch the game. The new catcher, Josh Gibson, went on to become the most celebrated power hitter in African American baseball history.[43]

In 1934, age finally caught up with Williams. Having lost some of his throwing speed and able to pitch for only an inning or two, he retired. He remained in New York, the site of so many of his pitching accomplishments, tending bar at the Harlem Grill.[44] He lived in the city for the remainder of his life.

Even in retirement, Williams stayed connected with black baseball. Through his job at the Harlem Grill, Williams convinced Buck Leonard, the power-hitting future Hall of Fame first baseman, to sign with the Homestead Grays. Then in 1934, after his retirement, Williams returned to the mound for the Homestead Grays on August 5 for a one-time pitching performance. As a part of "Smokey Joe Williams Day," Williams pitched two scoreless innings at Forbes Field in Pittsburg against an interracial semi-professional team sponsored by the Berghoff Brewing Company of Fort Wayne, Indiana.[45]

In 1950, Williams's importance to the game was recognized when the New York Giants of the National League honored the seventy-four-year-old pitcher with his own day at the Polo Grounds. Reporters asked Williams for his opinion on baseball's recent integration, and if he felt any bitterness over never playing in the white major leagues. Williams responded with a quick "no." "The important thing," he said, "is that the long fight is over. I praise the Lord I've lived to see the day."[46] Several weeks later, "Smokey" Joe Williams, the greatest African American pitcher ever to play the game, passed away. In 1999, in recognition of everything he accomplished in baseball, the Veterans Committee for the National Baseball Hall of Fame chose "Smokey" Joe Williams for enshrinement.[47]

Another Texan who shaped African American baseball, as well as helped define black masculinity and the Texas African American community, was Raleigh "Biz" Mackey, the game's greatest defensive catcher. Born in Eagle Pass, Texas, in 1897, Mackey changed the defensive requirements for catchers and established skills and techniques still used today by catchers to control games. While equipped with all the physical and intellectual talents needed behind the plate for strategy in calling pitches and plays, Mackey's greatest attribute was his powerful throwing arm. Most catchers chose to

Raleigh "Biz" Mackey,
one of the most dominant
catchers in Negro League
history. National Baseball
Hall of Fame Library,
Cooperstown, N.Y.

stand up to throw to a base in order to get more force behind the throw. Even from the weaker position on his knees, Mackey still regularly threw out runners.[48]

In addition to his superb natural abilities, Mackey also established himself as one of the most studious players in black baseball. He analyzed the art of hitting, as well as other aspects of the game. He memorized the weaknesses of his opponents at the plate and the strong points of his pitchers. Using this knowledge, he made his pitchers better by calling pitches and locations that favored their skills and at the same time targeted the hitters' weaknesses. Mackey also understood human nature, allowing him to control the temperament of his pitchers and thus make them even more effective.[49] He passed this scientific approach to catching on to other players, and it eventually became the norm for how both white and black catchers approached the game. At this time in the United States African Americans, and especially African American males, were portrayed as unintelligent. Mackey's cerebral approach to calling baseball games and pitches added a strong intellectual component to images of black masculinity.

Mackey's one great weakness, though, was a fondness for alcohol. He regularly played drunk. If an opponent smelled liquor on Mackey during a game, the other team attempted to steal bases more often. Even when inebriated, Mackey's natural ability proved great enough to throw out the majority of base runners who tried to steal on him.[50] Chet Brewer said about Mackey's drinking, "He'd party all night and go out to the ball park at ten o'clock in the morning, take a shower, and come out and catch a double header."[51]

Mackey began his baseball career with a Prairie League team in Luling, Texas. In 1918, he joined the San Antonio Black Aces and quickly became their star. Unfortunately, the team disbanded in 1920 because of financial problems.[52] When the Black Aces folded, Mackey and seven other San Antonio players saw their contracts sold to the Indianapolis ABCs. Indianapolis already had a catcher, who was also the team's veteran captain, so Mackey served as a utility player, playing whatever position the team needed. In his three years with the ABCs, Mackey recorded batting averages of .306, .296, and .361, along with slugging percentages of .558 and .630.[53] In 1923 he left the ABCs for more money, and the potential opportunity to catch, with the Philadelphia Hilldales of the new Eastern Colored League.

Mackey exhibited a hitting prowess almost as great as his defensive skills. He compiled a .335 lifetime batting average and hit .326 in fourteen games against white major league players.[54] In 1923 he hit .364 and led Philadelphia to the Eastern Colored League crown. The next year he hit .363, again leading his team to the league title. Unfortunately, the Hilldales lost to the Kansas City Monarchs in nine games in the first-ever Negro World Series. Cumberland Posey recalled, "For combined hitting, thinking, throwing, and physical endowment, there has never been another like Biz Mackey."[55]

Despite the great performances by Mackey at bat and behind the plate, Philadelphia already had a star catcher in fellow Texan Louis Santop. To keep Mackey's bat in the lineup, the Daisies played him at any open position. For the first Colored World Series in 1924, Mackey mostly played shortstop.[56] In the 1925 championship series, however, Mackey won the position of catcher outright. For the next two decades he never relinquished his spot, setting the standard for how to play the position.[57]

Once as a member of the Philadelphia Hilldales, Mackey decided he wanted to test his arm strength against the base-stealing ability of James "Cool Papa" Bell, the fastest man ever to play African American baseball. Mackey formulated a plan to throw out Bell, which he then shared with his pitcher, Walter MacDonald. With Bell on first base, Mackey called three straight pitchouts. MacDonald threw the ball intentionally high. This caused Mackey to stand up to catch the pitch, placing him in a perfect position to throw the ball to second base. Bell, thinking the pitcher dared not give three straight balls to the batter, broke to steal second base on the third high pitch. The plan worked perfectly. With Mackey already in position, the Texas catcher threw out Bell with relative ease, something that almost never happened.[58]

Flaunting his skills behind the plate, Mackey never took off his mask on pop-ups to see the ball better. He also helped his pitchers get called strikes from the umpires by moving his body to make the pitches look better. If the pitcher threw the ball low, Mackey raised his body. If the pitch came in high, he lowered his body. Because of his body movement, Mackey fooled the home plate umpires into thinking the catcher's mitt never moved, only Mackey's body. The movements also made the pitches appear to come straight down the middle of the plate instead of being high or low. As a result, umpires called more strikes when Mackey caught.[59] This art of deception became a stock practice for catchers in both black and white baseball.

Mackey also excelled at using psychology on opposing batters as a means of taking them out of their games and thus decreasing their effectiveness at the plate. He carried on all kinds of conversations with the batters while they were trying to hit. He would use humor, tease the batters good naturedly, and carry on conversations concerning every imaginable topic except baseball in an effort to distract opponents. Buck Leonard remembered that Mackey would ask a player what kind of bat he used, and then tell the umpire he doubted that the player's bat was legal. "Just anything to upset you," said Leonard.[60]

In recognition of his ability, Mackey received an invitation to go with a team of black all-stars on a barnstorming tour of Japan. The trip, which took place in 1927, occurred seven years before Babe Ruth and a team of white all-stars embarked on their famous tour of the country. The trip marked the first time many Japanese citizens saw a black person. Playing against Japanese college teams, the African American players lost only one game.[61] After each day's contest concluded, the black players put on skills exhibitions in order to entertain the Japanese fans. The Negro League stars went through the "shadow ball" drill, a pantomime game performed without a ball. The African American players also put on exhibitions of base running and hitting. Mackey showed off his ability to throw to second base from a squatting position. He also became the first player to hit a baseball out of Japan's new Meiji Shrine Stadium, one of the largest stadiums in the country.[62]

After the tour of Japan ended, Mackey returned to the Philadelphia Hilldales. He stayed with the Hilldales until the team and the Eastern Negro League both folded in 1930. For the next three years Mackey changed teams regularly and played sporadically, mainly in exhibition games.[63]

In 1933, he signed to play with the Philadelphia Stars of the new Negro National League. While with the Stars, Mackey was elected by the Negro League fans to be the starting catcher for the East squad in the inaugural East-West All-Star Game, beating out the legendary power hitter Josh Gibson. Despite being thirty-six years old in 1933, an advanced age for a professional baseball player, Mackey still exhibited the best defensive skills as a catcher. As a result, he received election to four of the first six East-

West games.[64] He also helped the Stars win the new Negro National League championship in 1934.

Among all of his accomplishments, it was with the Stars that Mackey made his greatest contribution through his discovery and training of a thirteen-year-old local boy named Roy Campanella. Mackey took the future member of the Hall of Fame under his wing and taught Campanella everything he knew about catching, including how to handle pitchers and the scientific study of opponents' weaknesses at the plate. In 1936, Mackey left Philadelphia to serve as the player-manager for the Baltimore Elite Giants. After joining Baltimore, he immediately signed the then sixteen-year-old Campanella to a contract. Campanella later explained: "I sat beside Mackey in the dugout. I relied on everything he told me."[65] In describing how well Campanella took to Mackey's teaching, Negro League star Judy Johnson claimed that if someone watched Campanella catch a game, they were actually watching Mackey, because Campanella used all of the skills and tricks he learned from his old manager and mentor.[66]

In 1939, Mackey left the Elite Giants and joined the Newark Eagles. With the Eagles, he continued to catch and manage, as well as tutor young players. Mackey trained such future stars of integrated baseball as Monte Irvin, Larry Doby, and Don Newcombe. Mackey also continued to put up impressive offensive numbers despite being over forty years old, hitting .307 in 1945. In 1946, he led the Eagles to a Negro World Series championship over the Kansas City Monarchs.[67]

In 1950, Mackey retired from baseball after thirty years and moved to Los Angeles where he lived the remainder of his years. In 1959, the Los Angeles Dodgers held a Roy Campanella Day, honoring their great catcher. When he came onto the field, Campanella brought Mackey with him. Campanella introduced Mackey as the man who taught him everything he knew.[68] Six years after receiving these accolades from Campanella and the Dodgers fans, Raleigh "Biz" Mackey passed away on September 22, 1965, in Los Angeles.[69] Baseball paid Mackey the ultimate honor in 2006 when a special Negro League committee elected him to the National Baseball Hall of Fame.

The third black Texan who played a major role in shaping the game of baseball, the African American community, and the national image of black masculinity was Willie Wells. Wells developed his skills on the sand-

Willie Wells, the best offensive and defensive shortstop in the Negro leagues during the 1930s and 1940s. National Baseball Hall of Fame Library, Cooperstown, N.Y.

lots of Austin, eventually earning recognition as the best shortstop in African American baseball history. For almost thirty years, Wells served as the model for the position. He was not a physically intimidating figure on the baseball field, standing only five feet, seven inches tall and weighing 160 pounds. Still, Wells hit for power and average, regularly batting over .320.[70]

As a fielder, Wells possessed good range and an accurate throwing arm, and he very rarely made an error. His knowledge of the shortstop position and the game of baseball proved his greatest assets as a shortstop. By studying opponents' tendencies at bat, Wells gave himself an advantage that allowed him to put out most batters. His ability to prevent base hits, as well as his power at the plate, landed Wells in eight East-West All-Star games, every all-time greatest list, and eventually in the National Baseball Hall of Fame. Author Art Rust, Jr., believed that "Willie Wells of the Newark Eagles probably was just as good as Marty Marion, Pee Wee Reese, or Phil Rizzuto."[71] Like Biz Mackey before him, Wells's reputation as an intelligent player and strategist augmented a positive image of black masculinity.

Born to a poor family in Austin on August 10, 1905, Wells began his baseball career in local pickup games.[72] As a youth during the early 1920s, he learned the fundamentals of baseball at Dodds Field. Wells went to the stadium regularly to watch the local semiprofessional black teams play. One time when Austin faced the team from San Antonio, Biz Mackey, who at the time played for the San Antonio Black Aces, noticed Wells hanging around the ballpark. Mackey called Wells over and struck up a conversation. Mackey recognized Wells's love for baseball and knowledge of the game, and as a result allowed the youth to carry the Aces' bags when the team played in the Texas capital. Mackey also worked with Wells on his hitting and throwing skills, as well as let the young man sit in the dugout with the Aces during games.[73]

The experience provided Wells with invaluable tutoring on the intricacies of baseball, knowledge he would apply later in life as a manager in the Negro leagues. When he developed as a player, Wells's ability as a hard-hitting shortstop earned him a spot on the Black Aces. In 1924, his second year with the team, they played several exhibition games against the Chicago American Giants and the St. Louis Stars, both of the Negro National League. Wells's skills at shortstop and at the plate impressed Rube Foster of the American Giants and Bill Wallace of St. Louis so much that both men wanted to sign him to a contract.[74]

When the two managers approached Wells's mother about the possibility of her son playing professional baseball, she adamantly refused. Mrs. Wells wanted her son, a graduate of Anderson High School, Austin's only black high school, to attend college.[75] Foster and Wallace both attempted to change her mind by offering her son contracts worth several hundred dollars a month. Given that Wells's previous jobs involved shucking corn and delivering newspapers, the contracts offered more money than he had ever seen in his life. His mother still refused. She stood her ground until both men promised that Wells could attend college in the off-season.[76]

Foster and Wallace both believed that once Wells experienced life in black professional baseball, he would lose the desire to attend college. With both managers optimistic about Wells joining their teams, they waited for him to make his decision. In the end, Wallace won. Mrs. Wells told her son to sign with the Stars because St. Louis was closer to Austin than Chicago.[77]

Despite all the effort to bring Wells into professional black baseball, he failed to make an immediate impact. Batting in the eighth position for the Stars, he found it difficult to hit Negro League curve balls. Once the inability of the highly touted rookie became well known, the Stars' opponents taunted Wells continually. When he came to bat, the other team's players yelled, "Hey Wells, here comes the curve ball."[78] He finished out the season with St. Louis, but returned to Austin in the off-season, enrolled at Samuel Huston College, a small black college, and assumed his baseball career was over.

Wells's college education lasted only a short time. Dick Redding, a star of the Negro leagues who played both pitcher and shortstop, suffered an injury during winter ball in California. Redding's team suddenly needed a replacement at shortstop. The members of the St. Louis Stars on the team remembered Wells and recommended him for the job.[79] Wells's mother still wanted her son to finish college, but as he recalled, "I looked at her taking in washing and ironing. 'Now I can help her,' I thought."[80] He never returned to college.

His second stint in professional black baseball proved more successful. Wells solved his batting problems and could now hit the curve ball. Through lots of practice and hard work, he transformed himself into a great hitter. Playing with St. Louis in 1926 and 1927, he hit .378 and .346, respectively. Also in 1926, Wells set a then Negro National League record for the most home runs in a single season, hitting twenty-seven in eighty-eight games. Wells's home run per game average equaled or bettered that of almost anyone in white baseball at the time, evidence that black masculinity was equal to white. Wells's prowess at the plate continued, as he won back-to-back Negro National League batting titles in 1929 and 1930 with averages of .368 and .404.[81]

While his hitting received considerable attention from fans and the black community in Texas, Wells also developed into the best defensive shortstop in black baseball. Pitcher Max Manning recalled that while Wells did not possess the strongest arm in the league, his quick throws to first always seemed to get opponents out by a step.[82] With Wells leading the way in the field and at the plate, the St. Louis Stars won the Negro National League pennant in 1928, 1930, and 1931.[83]

After the 1931 season, Wells's playing days with the St. Louis Stars came to an end when the Negro National League folded. Wells suddenly found himself in search of a team. He bounced around African American baseball, playing for the Detroit Wolves, Homestead Grays, and Kansas City Monarchs, all in 1932. Late in the season, he joined the Chicago American Giants. In his first two seasons as the starting shortstop for the American Giants, Wells led the team to consecutive championships, winning the Negro Southern League pennant in 1932 and the new Negro National League championship in 1933.[84]

Wells continued his superb hitting, posting an average of .300 in 1933. Because of his success at the plate, as well as his unmatched skill at shortstop, the African American fans elected Wells the starting shortstop for the West team in the first annual East-West All-Star game. In the game, Wells registered two hits, leading his team to victory. On seven other occasions he started at shortstop in the East-West game.[85] In 1934 alone, he received 48,000 votes, a considerable number for the time, and an accomplishment recounted by the black press and fans in Texas.[86]

In 1936, Wells demonstrated his integrity and commitment to his teammates. Robert Cole, the owner of the Chicago American Giants, offered Wells a bribe. With the American Giants experiencing financial difficulties, Cole wanted to save money by not paying his players a salary. Instead he proposed to pay players by passing a hat among the fans at the team's home games. The players would then divide up the money that remained after all team expenses were paid. Cole offered Wells a raise if Wells convinced the other American Giants players to go along with the deal. Wells refused, quit the team in protest, and signed with the Newark Eagles.[87] Since the incident took place in the middle of the Great Depression, Wells received considerable praise from African Americans throughout the country. In standing up to the team owner, Wells symbolized many people's own plight and desire to stand up to business management.

As the shortstop for the Newark Eagles, Wells, along with third baseman Ray Dandridge, second baseman Dick Seay, and first baseman "Mule" Suttles, made up a group known as the "million dollar infield."[88] Possibly the best defensive infield in the history of African American baseball, the group acquired its name from the claim that, if white, the salaries of the four players would have equaled a million dollars. No combination of players, white or black, ever covered the left side of the infield as successfully as Wells and Dandridge. They performed so well together that they worked strategies to complement each of their abilities. For example, when Wells fielded a ground ball deep in the hole between shortstop and third base, he would toss the ball to Dandridge, who possessed the stronger arm and subsequently threw the runner out at first base.[89]

Wells batted over .340 from 1936 to 1940. In recognition of his hitting, the Spalding Company, who manufactured sporting goods, allowed him to select the wood for his bats and built them to his specifications. The major sporting goods companies usually gave these privileges only to major leaguers.[90]

Wells was a part of other innovations that shaped baseball. To aid his fielding, Wells cut a hole in the palm of his glove and removed the padding. While this modification was less comfortable for his hand, it gave him greater flexibility than could be had with the heavily stuffed gloves of the time. The modification enabled him to handle ground balls better, thus reducing errors.[91] Wells's less padded, more flexible mitt proved the predecessor to the modern baseball glove.

In 1937, Wells became the player-manager of the Newark Eagles, a position he held for the next three years and from where he further shaped African American baseball. Respected by his players, Wells tutored several future stars. In one act as manager, he moved two rookie infielders, Monte Irvin and Larry Doby, to the outfield. Both men went on to have Hall of Fame careers in the integrated major leagues at their new positions.[92]

In the off-season, Wells continued to play baseball, competing in the Cuban League. The fact that he returned each winter allowed Wells to establish a large following in Latin America. In 1940, Mexican millionaire Jorge Pasqual wanted his Vera Cruz team to win the Mexican League championship; so he signed several of the best players in black baseball, including Willie Wells.[93] Playing for Vera Cruz in 1940 and 1941, Wells posted batting averages of .345 and .347. His team also won the Mexican League pennant in 1940. While playing in Mexico, Wells received the nickname of "El Diablo" from the fans for his dominance at the position of shortstop.[94]

Playing in Mexico brought a new freedom for African American baseball players and highlighted the racial discrimination in the United States. Wells and the other black players lived in affluent neighborhoods, made high salaries, and experienced none of the racial prejudices that existed in U.S. baseball. Wells later described his experience in Mexico: "I've found freedom and democracy here, something I never found in the United States. I was branded a Negro in the states and had to act accordingly. Everything I did, including playing ball, was regarded by my color. Well here in Mexico I am a man. I can go as far in baseball as I am capable."[95]

When the United States entered World War II in 1942, Wells wrote Abe Manley, owner of the Newark Eagles, and offered to return to the team, but only as player-manager and only if he received a salary of three hundred fifteen dollars a month. Manley, happy over the return of his star shortstop, even if it was at the advanced age of thirty-seven, agreed to the contract demand. In his first year back, Wells hit .361. The same year, Cum Posey, owner of the Homestead Grays and writer for the *Pittsburgh Courier*, named Wells to his annual All American Negro League dream team. In 1943, however, Wells got into an argument with Effa Manley, Abe's wife and part-owner of the team, and quit the Eagles. Wells returned to Mexico, where he stayed for the next two years.[96]

In 1942, before leaving the Newark Eagles for Mexico, Wells created what became his longest lasting contribution to the game of baseball, the batting helmet. Wells first wore a modified miner's helmet for protection in a game in 1939. Three years later, Bill Byrd, a pitcher for the Baltimore Elite Giants hit Wells in the head with a pitch, knocking him unconscious. Doctors told Wells to rest a few weeks and not play. He refused, continued to play, and one week later the Eagles again faced Baltimore and Byrd. Wells came to bat wearing a workman's hardhat modified with an earflap to protect his head. His use of the homemade contraption made him the first baseball player, black or white, to wear a batting helmet.[97]

Wells played in Mexico for the next couple of years. With World War II coming to an end, though, Wells returned to the United States and African

American baseball in 1944. Over the next ten years, he bounced around from team to team, playing for the Chicago American Giants, New York Black Yankees, Baltimore Elite Giants, Indianapolis Clowns, Memphis Red Sox, and Birmingham Black Barons. While no longer as quick in the field, Wells still put up impressive numbers at the plate, batting .328 at the age of forty-three in 1948.[98]

Wells also worked as a manager during the late 1940s. While managing the Memphis Red Sox in 1949, Wells inserted himself into several games. By participating in the games, he played with his son, Willie Wells, Jr. With Wells, Sr., playing second base and Wells, Jr., at shortstop, the two men became the first father and son to play together on the same team in professional baseball history. They also made up the only father and son double-play combination, ever, a fact the Texas black press took pleasure in bringing to the attention of fans.[99]

In 1954, Wells retired from baseball after twenty-eight years. He finished his career with a lifetime batting average of .364 against other black teams, and a .410 average against white major leaguers. Buck O'Neil, the longtime Negro League player and manager, described Wells's play, saying: "He could hit to all fields, hit with power, bunt, and stretch singles into doubles and doubles into triples. But it was his glove that truly dazzled. . . . Old-timers in St. Louis who saw Willie play for the St. Louis Stars still have not seen his equal."[100]

After his retirement, Wells owned a delicatessen in New York City for seventeen years. In 1973, he returned to Austin, Texas, where he cared for his ailing mother. After she passed away, he continued to live in the house in which he had grown up until his own death in 1989.[101] In 1998, Wells was inducted into the National Baseball Hall of Fame. In recognition of this ultimate honor, his hometown of Austin declared February 6, 1998, "Willie Wells Day." His daughter Stella Wells spoke at a ceremony honoring her father. The city renamed Congress Avenue "Willie Wells Avenue" for the day. [102]

Wells received other posthumous recognitions. In 2003, Carsey Walker, Jr., performed as Wells in a one-man play written by Robi Polgar. The play, *The Willie Wells Story*, appeared at the Bob Bullock Texas State History Museum in Austin as a part of the museum's exhibit Play Ball! Texas Baseball. The following year, Gary Roberts, an Austin native, worked with Wells's daughter; the Round Rock Express, a local minor league team; and the Texas State Cemetery to transfer Wells's remains from Evergreen Cemetery to the Texas State Cemetery. The October 2004 ceremony brought more than one hundred people, including then Texas governor Rick Perry, to watch as Wells became only the second African American buried in the cemetery.[103] These posthumous honors were fitting tributes to a Texan who helped define for a nation the Texas black community and who left an indelible mark on African American baseball history.

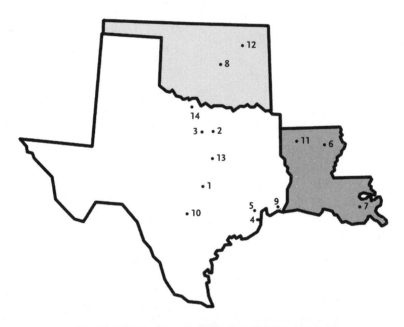

**Member Towns of the
Texas-Oklahoma-Louisiana League**

1. Austin	8. Oklahoma City
2. Dallas	9. Port Arthur
3. Fort Worth	10. San Antonio
4. Galveston	11. Shreveport
5. Houston	12. Tulsa
6. Monroe	13. Waco
7. New Orleans	14. Wichita Falls

Courtesy of Mike Jones

The Texas-Oklahoma-Louisiana League

PROFESSIONAL BLACK BASEBALL COMES TO TEXAS

5 As African American baseball players from Texas achieved star status in professional black baseball, black baseball in Texas also gained national recognition. Teams from the Negro National League, the Eastern Negro League, and the Negro Southern League scheduled exhibitions against Texas squads. More and more black teams appeared around Texas. The importance of the game to the Texas black community as a force of identity and cultural pride grew with the number of teams playing baseball. The popularity and influence of the game in the state reached its peak in 1929 with the creation of the professional Texas-Oklahoma-Louisiana League (TOL). Built on the foundation created by years of semiprofessional baseball and by such men as Rube Foster, the TOL proved Texas black baseball was equal to that of anywhere else in the country. Furthermore, the professional status of the TOL allowed the black teams in Texas to shape the game of baseball and its history even more.

The new African American league began when Quincy J. Gilmore, secretary of the Negro National League and president of the Kansas City Monarchs, issued a press release on January 12, 1929, announcing his interest in forming a professional black baseball league in the American Southwest. Immediately after declaring his intentions, Gilmore left for the states of

Texas, Oklahoma, and Louisiana to invite several teams to join his new league, which would be known as the Texas-Oklahoma-Louisiana League. He offered franchises to Tulsa, Oklahoma City, Dallas, Fort Worth, Houston, San Antonio, Waco, Galveston, Beaumont, and Shreveport. Optimistic about his new league, Gilmore declared, "I believe that with my experience in the game and the natural love for baseball in the South, that organized baseball will go big down there."[1]

One week later, on Tuesday, January 22, Gilmore met with representatives from teams interested in joining the league in what the *Houston Informer* called the "largest gathering of Negro baseball men ever brought together in the South."[2] Gilmore, along with baseball men from Tulsa, Oklahoma City, Dallas, Fort Worth, Shreveport, Houston, San Antonio, and Wichita Falls, held a conference at the Pythian Temple in Dallas, the local home of a black fraternal organization. At the meeting, Gilmore laid out his plans. The men present voted unanimously in favor of the proposal, thus officially creating the Texas-Oklahoma-Louisiana League.[3] The creation of the league was a source of pride for the African American community in Texas.

The TOL's charter followed closely the operating procedures of Rube Foster's Negro National League. Each team played a split schedule, consisting of one hundred games divided into two halves. A winner was declared for each half. For playing facilities, each team was responsible for contracting the use of a local stadium.[4]

The team representatives at the meeting elected Gilmore president of the new league for a term of five years. Gilmore then established the Pythian Temple in Dallas as the league's headquarters. Along with electing a league president, the men present filled the remainder of the TOL's officer positions. J. B. Grigsby, director of the American Mutual Benefit Association, a black insurance group in Houston, became the vice president.[5] Edgar Crawford of Tulsa was elected second vice president. The team representatives also named Henry Strickland, owner of the *Dallas Express* and founder of the Excelsior Life Insurance Company of Dallas, to the position of treasurer.[6] Other officers included William Grace of Tulsa, E. F. Nuns of Shreveport, and William Tresivant of Fort Worth, who became the league commissioners. F. T. Alexander of Oklahoma City became chairman of the board of directors. A. S. Wells, a prominent Dallas attorney who would run for the Fourteenth District Court in Dallas in 1935, served as legal advisor for the TOL.[7] They also established one more position, that of medical examiner, who was not, as the name suggests, a coroner, but responsible for protecting the health of the league players.[8]

Before the meeting ended, Gilmore called for a second meeting to take place in Dallas on February 24. He wanted to set the official schedule for the upcoming season, as well as to admit four new teams to the league: Galveston, Austin, Beaumont, and Waco. For the second meeting, Gilmore wanted representatives of each city to bring their local African American newspaper reporters in order to inform the public of the league, as well as to begin to build fan support. Gilmore concluded the meeting by issuing a formal request to the two existing black professional leagues, the Negro National League and the Eastern Negro League, to honor the TOL's contracts and players and not sign away TOL players.[9]

As the TOL teams prepared for the meeting on February 24, President Gilmore mailed player contracts to all the team owners. He hoped that every team would have its players signed by the meeting in February. In regard to this, the league executives also issued a statement saying that TOL members refused to recruit players from any team, whether they were other prominent teams or local semiprofessional teams, without first receiving the permission of the other team's owners.[10] This statement was designed to foster good will between the TOL and existing teams in the states.

Each TOL team officially completed all the preparations by securing the use of a baseball park in which to play. All but two of the league teams contracted with local white-owned parks. Even though the TOL teams used the stadiums only on weekends when the white teams played out of town, these stadiums were a vast improvement over the facilities that many African American baseball players in the South were used to. In Texas, the TOL teams played in the parks, such as Houston's Buffalo Stadium, used by the members of the Texas League, a minor league affiliated with the white major leagues.[11]

Two teams, Shreveport and Dallas, used stadiums owned entirely by African Americans. In Shreveport, the Black Sports played in a facility nicer and larger than the white Texas League park in the city. The Dallas Black Giants played their games in a stadium with a seating capacity of ten thousand, one of the largest in the country. Several years earlier, when the local white team's park burned, the white Dallas Giants rented the black stadium, a rare event in baseball.[12] The black press in Texas excitedly retold the plight of the white Giants, since this reversed the usual racial scenario of the black team being at the mercy of the white for playing time.

Other league decisions made before the February meeting centered on day-to-day logistics, such as umpires and travel. Gilmore wanted to use only African American umpires in all TOL games. Therefore, the executive board named four official league umpires to work the 1929 season. The job description for these official umpires called for one of them to supervise a team of local umpires at every league game. Sadly, no record exists of these first umpires, their pay, or how they managed to cover fifty games in five cities during the inaugural season. As for team travel, the TOL clubs agreed to use private cars or buses, thus saving the league money on train fare. Finally, Gilmore announced the league had obtained contracts for the season's supply of baseballs, all of which carried the league's logo and his name as president, a practice used by the white major leagues.[13]

At the February 24 meeting, President Gilmore and the other league officials put the finishing touches on the Texas-Oklahoma-Louisiana League. With the majority of the day-to-day operations already completed, the meeting served mainly to raise awareness of, and enthusiasm for, the TOL. The plan to create fan excitement involved inviting the Texas black press and African American baseball men from around the country to the meeting. These men in turn reported the proceedings to the rest of the country. The guests in attendance included Clarence Starks of the *Dallas Express*; H. D. English of Texas College, a historically black college in Tyler; J. L. Wilkinson of the Kansas City Monarchs; and Albert White, who covered the proceedings for both the white and black newspapers in Shreveport, Louisiana.[14] By working to obtain support among black Texans, the league officials hoped to accomplish two things. First, they wanted to establish the TOL as an institution of community pride and cultural identity for African Americans. Each team served as a symbol of the town in which it played, and in turn allowed for boosterism. Second, the league officials sought to establish fan support for the teams as a means of ensuring attendance and financial success.

At the March meeting, Dallas, Wichita Falls, Houston, Shreveport, Tulsa, Oklahoma City, San Antonio, and Fort Worth all received franchises as the first official TOL members, while Waco and Galveston fell out. The league chose these towns because of their large African American populations, ranging from fourteen thousand in Oklahoma City to sixty-three thousand in Houston.[15] The large populations obviously increased the likelihood of high attendance numbers. Furthermore, to increase fan recognition and support, each TOL team took the name of the local white Texas League team and added the word *black*. Finally, Gilmore fixed April 27 as opening day for the 1929 season. To boost enthusiasm, he informed all in attendance that "elaborate preparations will soon be under way to make this season's opening the largest and most outstanding ever seen by any Negro baseball league."[16] His statement was passed on to the Texas African American community by the black newspapermen in attendance.

Over the next month, all the members of the league made their final preparations for the inaugural season. The league executive committee called for another meeting on March 24 to complete the schedule for the season. In San Antonio, Hayes Pendergraph, a prominent local business-man, took over control of the Black Indians, hiring as manager Bob Pat-terson, formerly of the Birmingham Black Barons. Ed Mason, whom the *Houston Informer* called "one of the best known baseball men in the South," took charge of the Wichita Falls Black Spudders.[17] The recognition of men connected with the Negro leagues further united the African American community in Texas with the national black culture and community.

Every TOL team owner sent out calls for players to report to their re-spective cities for spring training.[18] But last-minute changes did occur. The Dallas Black Giants, who played in a large black-owned stadium, suddenly found it unusable. The city of Dallas began building new dikes to assist with the city's water supply. The dikes ran through the middle of River-side Park, the Black Giants' stadium. The team compensated by obtaining the use of the white Texas League park in Dallas. The loss of an African American–owned facility, and the subsequent dependence on a white-owned ball park, exacerbated the feelings of black Dallasites toward white city officials. The league's schedule committee met on March 24 to final-ize the 1929 schedule. Using the date previously decided on by President Gilmore, the committee set opening day for the first half of the season as April 27, with the second half beginning on July 4. Special consideration in scheduling went to the Texas teams, allowing them to play home games on June 19. Known as Juneteenth, the holiday marked the day Texas slaves received their emancipation following the Civil War. Because white parks were often being used, the committee scheduled games only for weekends and Mondays that the white teams played out of town. As a result, the TOL teams played a doubleheader every Sunday and one game on Mondays.[19] This scheduling pattern allowed as many black fans as possible to attend games, since the majority had only Sundays off from work. Furthermore, Sunday and Monday games allowed the players the opportunity to work part-time jobs during the week to supplement their income, or play with local semiprofessionals or in a city league during the week. Competing on these extra teams further built community support and recognition of the TOL as a source of cultural pride and racial identity. After the schedule was finalized, the Texas-Oklahoma-Louisiana League finally stood ready to begin its first season.

As a tune-up for the upcoming season, and as a means to create more public exposure, the Houston Black Buffaloes faced the Prairie View Panthers in two exhibition games. Prairie View College, the largest African American college in the state, had a significant fan base, especially in the Houston area. Competing against Prairie View united the TOL with the existing support for the school. Houston swept the series, winning the first game 18 to 4 and the second game 3 to 1. The second game proved to be a competitive contest. Asa Hilliard, the Panther's pitcher, allowed the Black Buffaloes only five hits and no earned runs. Unfortunately, errors by Hilliard's teammates cost Prairie View the game.[20]

When opening day arrived, enthusiasm ran high. The Dallas, Fort Worth, and Houston clubs all made elaborate preparations for an opener that celebrated the state's black community. Texas businesses also got involved, as local railroad companies ran special trains to the three cities, hoping to encourage fans from around the state to attend. One of these chartered trains left San Antonio for Houston on Saturday, carrying not only fans but also a fifty-piece band and a representative of the mayor's office.[21] The use of special trains for fans to attend games was a common occurrence in both black and white college football at the time.

In Dallas, the black citizens held a motor parade through the city, with numerous African American businesses and fraternal organizations represented. During the game, the same black groups held parties in the stadium's box seats. To help encourage attendance, the city of Dallas declared a half-day holiday, closing all African American businesses at noon.[22]

To kick off the game between the Forth Worth Black Panthers and the Wichita Falls Black Spudders, the Fort Worth Boosters Club decorated all of the shops in the African American business district with signs and banners. At the Fort Worth stadium, a brass band gave a concert between innings for the fans' enjoyment.[23] Also, W. M. McDonald, a black Fort Worth political leader, civil rights activist, and secretary of the Prince Hall Free and Accepted Masons, threw out the first pitch.[24]

All of these efforts helped unite the league and teams with the Texas black community, as well as improved attendance. Fans turned out in the hundreds to usher in the inaugural season of the TOL. In Houston, what the *Informer* claimed to be "the largest crowd ever to witness an African American baseball game in the city's history," including league president Quincy J. Gilmore, watched the Houston Black Buffaloes lose to the San Antonio Black Indians, 5 to 4.[25] The game was not one of the most technically perfect games ever played, unfortunately, as San Antonio scored all of its runs off Houston errors.

Near the end of the game, an ugly situation marred the opening-day festivities. Several members of the Black Indians objected to a decision by umpire Richard Ponder. The argument became so heated that Houston police officers came onto the field and escorted San Antonio's manager, Thomas Calloway, out of the stadium.[26] Gilmore dealt with the problem immediately in order to prevent any such future events. He officially expressed his disapproval of San Antonio's actions and stated that if such behavior occurred again, San Antonio's team would be suspended from the league.[27]

Houston and San Antonio split a doubleheader on Monday, April 29, allowing San Antonio to win the inaugural series two games to one. Despite the loss, Houston's fans remained extremely excited about their team and the TOL, turning out in large numbers for games. Having a professional black team was a source of pride for the African American community of each city in the league. It also allowed for boosterism and claims of equality with large, northern cities like Chicago and Pittsburgh that housed well-known Negro League teams.

The Black Buffaloes' next series of games occurred the following week in Shreveport, Louisiana. As if stimulated by the high fan turnout for the first set of games, attendance figures reached into the low thousands; the Southern Pacific Railroad ran a special train from Houston to Shreveport for the Sunday game. Using the Houston East and West Texas Railway, the charter train left Houston Saturday night, May 4, and returned the next night following the game.[28]

After the first two weeks of the season, the Texas-Oklahoma-Louisiana League proved highly competitive. The Tulsa Black Oilers jumped out to a quick lead with a record of four wins and no loses. The next five teams, Houston, San Antonio, Dallas, Fort Worth, and Oklahoma City, all posted win-loss records of at least .500.[29]

Not every team played well in the beginning of the season. Two teams, Wichita Falls and Shreveport, started out poorly. To assist the Wichita Falls Black Spudders, who won only two of their first seven games, the league promised to move some players from other TOL teams to make the team competitive. The Shreveport Black Sports, who occupied last place with a record of one win and five losses, hired a new manager, Lem Hawkins, former first baseman of the Kansas City Monarchs and Chicago American Giants, in an attempt to turn their record around.[30]

As the 1929 season progressed, the initial excitement over the new league faded and attendance decreased for many of the teams. In an effort to boost fan attendance, Ernest Grigsby, secretary of the Black Buffaloes, moved all of Houston's games from Buffalo Stadium, the white Texas League stadium, to West End Park, an older stadium closer to the African American section of town. Buffalo Stadium existed on the edge of Houston's Third Ward, while West End Park was situated in the center of the city's Fourth Ward. Grigsby believed the central location of West End Park within the African American neighborhoods of the city would lead more people to attend games. West End Park also offered more affordable rent.[31]

Another problem for the TOL involved publicity and the keeping of accurate standings. Every team was to send daily reports of their games to the league office. Gilmore wanted these official documents to include every game's complete scoring. Unfortunately, not every team submitted their reports, and some of those that made it to the league office failed to include all the necessary information.[32]

Gilmore used these materials to keep the black press and the public updated on TOL happenings. This way the fans knew the players, expressed more interest in the teams, and came to identify with the teams as a part of the community. Attendance would rise, and fans would gladly pay the one-dollar ticket price, a considerable sum for the time considering the price of tickets to most black semiprofessional games was less than a dollar, with some games even being free. With no accounting for all the games played, no accurate league standings existed. Gilmore came up with a plan to alleviate this problem.[33]

Beginning on June 1, he assigned a publicity man to each team. This person had the sole responsibility of recording every home game his team played. At the end of a game, he made four copies of the box score he had just created, one for each of the teams involved in the contest, one for his own records, and one for the league office. The job description required the publicity men to mail their box score to the league president the same night as the game, sending it by special delivery via either Western Union or Postal Telegraph. Through this plan, Gilmore hoped to compile an accurate record of games played and the league standings.[34] Unfortunately, the time it took to copy the box scores, as well as the expense of sending several deliveries to numerous places, discouraged many of the publicity men from meeting their deadlines.

Despite its problems, the TOL did put on some exciting baseball games in its first season. In one game in Tulsa, Oklahoma, between the Tulsa Black Oilers and the San Antonio Black Indians, a racially mixed crowd, with whites sitting on one side of the bleachers and African Americans on the other, watched the two teams battle for fifteen innings. San Antonio and Tulsa took a two-run tie into extra innings. In the thirteenth inning, San Antonio appeared about to win, scoring one run, but Tulsa answered in the bottom of the inning, prolonging the game. Finally, in the fifteenth inning, San Antonio scored and then blanked Tulsa in their last at-bat, winning the game 4 to 3. Between innings, the African American fans danced and cheered as a band performed.[35]

As the first half of the 1929 season progressed, a new problem surfaced, one that the league officials had no means of dealing with: the weather. Rain caused the cancellation of eight games through June. Since the TOL teams played in white league parks on the white teams' days off, there was no way to make up canceled games.[36] As a result, the teams did not play the same number of contests during the season, making accurate standings difficult. For example, Houston finished in first place for the first half of the season, but played three fewer games than second-place San Antonio.

A large difference in the caliber of the teams also appeared. Only three of the league's eight teams, Houston, San Antonio, and Tulsa, finished the first half with winning records. The two last-place teams lost more than twenty of their first thirty games. The winning teams found it easy to attract fans. The ones with losing records, though, found themselves forced to look for ways to change their luck and boost attendance. The Dallas Black Giants, who finished the first half of the season with a record of eight wins and twenty-one losses, acquired an entirely new starting lineup for the second half.[37] The Wichita Falls team, located in the smallest city in the league with the smallest black population, finished in last place, winning only eight of thirty-four games, and attracted minuscule crowds. As a result, President Gilmore warned that, unless the Black Spudders' attendance and play improved, the team would be moved to Galveston, a larger city with a more extensive African American population.[38]

Another problem the league addressed at the beginning of the second half of the season was the ability of the umpires. The TOL wanted to use only African American umpires. Because no opportunities existed to train them, they learned the rules and how to enforce them on the job during league games. As a result, they made some bad calls, irritating the fans. Gilmore issued a statement asking fans to have patience, because the umpires performed a difficult job and tried their best.[39] The African American fans, being paying customers, continued to criticize.

The second half of the 1929 season began the way the first half had ended. Houston and Tulsa fought for first place, while Wichita Falls kept a tight grip on last place. The Fort Worth Black Panthers offered the only early surprise, opening the second half with a record of seven wins and one loss. Houston strengthened its lineup for a run at the second-half pennant through the addition of Chester Williams, a second baseman who had previously played in the Negro National League.[40]

Any hopes for an exciting pennant race in the second half of the 1929 season soon evaporated. The Houston Black Buffaloes, led by a dominant left-handed pitcher whom the black press referred to only by his last name of Foster, ran away with the pennant. The teams that finished in the bottom of the league saw their attendance figures dwindle to almost nothing. As the season came to an end and fan support waned, coverage of the league by the Texas African American press also decreased. The *Houston Informer* offered no coverage of the TOL during the entire month of August and most of September. The decline in fan support coincided with the beginning of the college football season, and football at Texas's historically black colleges was a major cultural institution and source of racial identity and pride. In Texas, come fall, everything placed second to college football.

By the end of September, the Houston Black Buffaloes clinched the second-half championship, giving them a clean sweep for the year. Gilmore used his connections with the Kansas City Monarchs, for whom he served as president for more than ten years, to organize a postseason series between Houston and the Negro National League champion Monarchs. Houston, the TOL, and the Texas black press proclaimed the competition as the battle for the "colored world's championship."⁴¹

The series between the Black Buffaloes and the Monarchs created great excitement in Houston and revived interest around the state for the league. The competition against the best team in the Negro leagues allowed African Americans in Texas to claim equality with the rest of the country. For African Americans nationally, Negro League baseball dominated the sports world. In Texas, where college football proved so important to identity, the sport was still mostly regional. TOL teams gave black Texans the opportunity to compete on the national level.

African Americans in Houston made elaborate plans for the upcoming series. A committee, headed up by local black businessman H. P. Carter, organized a parade and flag-raising ceremony before the first game. The parade moved through the streets of Houston, arriving at West End Park, where the series took place, at one o'clock in the afternoon. At the stadium, representatives of Houston's local fraternal organizations raised the American flag while a band played the national anthem. Finally, as the presidents of both leagues and other local celebrities looked on, L. B. Kinchion, grand chancellor of the Colored Knights of Pythias, threw out the first pitch. The league hired the Teal Portrait Studio, a prominent black-owned photography studio and school of photography in Houston, whose "status among black photographers is legendary," to record the game.⁴² In addition to taking still pictures, Teal also captured all the proceedings as a motion picture for viewing by fans who did not attend the game.⁴³ Unfortunately, none of these photographic records survive.

As the excitement over the series grew, other companies became involved in attracting fans to the games, as well as exploiting the opportunity to make money from the series. The Missouri Pacific Railroad offered special round-trip fares for fans who wanted to attend the games played in Houston. Paying one cent per mile, fans came from all over Texas to watch.⁴⁴

Thousands of fans packed West End Park on September 21 for the first game. The Buffaloes batted well, scoring twelve runs on twenty hits. Unfortunately, Kansas City put on an even greater hitting display, scoring fifteen runs on twenty-seven hits off Houston's top pitcher. The second game of the series proved more competitive than the first, as the Monarchs won a pitchers' duel, 3 to 2.[45]

Kansas City also won the next two games, by scores of 6 to 1 and 10 to 1, sweeping the series in four games. On September 28, in the third contest of the series, an altercation between Chester Williams, Houston's third baseman, and an African American umpire by the name of Gholston marred the game. In the seventh inning, Williams became angry over a call made by Gholston at third base, and he responded by hitting the official. The Houston police and Black Buffalo player-manager Roy Parnell, a native of the city who had returned to Houston from the Birmingham Black Barons with more than twenty years' experience, prevented a full-scale fight between Houston's players and the umpires. Gholston immediately ejected Williams and play resumed. One inning later, though, when Parnell came to bat, Gholston ejected him also for an unknown reason, causing more arguments between the Houston players and the umpires. The incident caused the promoters of the series to use two white umpires the next day in an effort to avoid further altercations.[46]

After Houston's loss to the Kansas City Monarchs in the self-proclaimed "colored world's championship," the Texas-Oklahoma-Louisiana League took the winter off. When March 1930 and spring training rolled around, the league underwent drastic changes. One major change consisted of the teams involved, as five of the original eight teams quit the league. Only Houston, San Antonio, and Shreveport returned for the second season. The league, which now went by the name of the Texas-Louisiana League (TL), gave franchises to Port Arthur, Waco, and New Orleans.[47]

These changes were prompted by the onset of the Great Depression. African Americans throughout the country felt the impact of the economic crisis. In baseball, organized black leagues and teams failed. The Negro National League closed in 1931. Touring teams like the Kansas City Monarchs played games against all comers in fields at fairgrounds, stadiums, and sandlots in an effort to survive.[48] Native Texan Willie Foster recalled the situation in African American baseball at the time, saying, "The people couldn't go to the ball game, and our bosses promised us so much money, but they didn't have it cause they weren't making it."[49] In Texas, African American unemployment rose from approximately 4 percent at the start of the 1930s to over 8 percent in 1933. Wages and family incomes fell as African Americans in rural areas lost access to agricultural land and urban blacks lost jobs.[50]

Despite the economic problems, as well as the major changes in league membership, the TL entered the 1930 season recognized as one of the top black professional leagues in the country, ranking just behind the Negro National League and Negro Southern League. The Kansas City Monarchs returned to Texas to play the Houston Black Buffaloes in a four-game spring training series.[51] The same month, the Homestead Grays, led by fifty-four-year-old pitcher and native Texan "Smokey" Joe Williams, made their first trip ever to the state, also to play the Black Buffaloes.[52] For blacks in the Lone Star State, recognition by the elite Negro teams continued to serve as a source of pride and community identity.

The 1930 season began favorably. The Dallas franchise, which returned to the league in place of Shreveport, which had dropped out less than a month before play began, swept Port Arthur in a two-game series to open the season in first place. One of the new teams, the Waco Black Cardinals, marked its TL debut by beating the San Antonio Black Indians two out of three games.[53] The loss of Shreveport made New Orleans the only team in the league not located in Texas.

As the season went on, Houston again ran away with the pennant. The Black Buffaloes dominated their opponents. In one series against Waco, Houston shut out the Black Cardinals in three straight games, scoring a total of twenty-four runs. In the series, Houston's pitcher, whom the newspaper referred to only as McHenry, pulled off an "iron man" performance by pitching both ends of a doubleheader.[54]

The problems of 1929 persisted in 1930. Teams continued to fail to report games to the league office, and bad weather again caused the league members to play an unequal number of games. One month into the season, first-place Houston had played twelve games, but second-place San Antonio only six.[55]

With the country experiencing increasing financial difficulties during the early days of the Great Depression, fan attendance at Texas-Louisiana League games remained low, with fewer than a thousand people regularly attending each contest. The league's executives tried the same promotions they had used the year before to attract fans, namely hiring bands to play between innings and making one game a week "Ladies' Night," where all women attended the game for free.[56] The executives knew that women would not attend the contests alone. So the teams would receive revenue from the ladies' escorts, as well as from the concessions purchased by couples.

Late in the 1930 season, the Houston Black Buffaloes tried another gimmick to draw in spectators. Beginning Saturday, August 2, they played all of their home games at night under floodlights.[57] The Black Buffaloes were not the first team in the country to use night baseball as a way to attract fans who worked during the day. That honor goes to the Kansas City Monarchs. In March 1930, Monarchs owner J. L. Wilkinson used a portable set of lights he ordered from the Giant Manufacturing Company of Omaha in a game in Lawrence, Kansas.[58] The use of lights by both the Monarchs and the Black Buffaloes occurred several years before the white major leagues adopted the practice. When the white Texas teams later began using lights, black Houstonians could point with pride to the fact that their team had played under lights first.

Unfortunately, these efforts to fill stadiums failed to make much of a difference. Attendance continued to decline steadily, and coverage of the league in the African American press also dwindled. From the beginning of May until the beginning of October, the *Houston Informer* published only two articles on the Texas-Louisiana League. Other major black newspapers in the state, like the *Dallas Express*, stopped publishing altogether. The lack of financial support for the Texas baseball teams illustrated an important point: regardless of how much cultural significance a sports team held for a community, the fans' financial concerns always proved more important. Some elements of black culture did flourish during the Depression. Duke Ellington made a considerable fortune off his music, while Zora Neale Hurston and Richard Wright wrote nationally acclaimed books. Their success, though, proved the exception to the norm. The works of Ellington, Hurston, and Wright, as well as that of a few others, were marketed nationally to both white and black audiences. African American sports did not have a similar support system, especially in southern states like Texas where the teams relied on their local community.

The Houston Black Buffaloes again won both halves of the season. Houston played the Chicago American Giants, champions of the Negro National League, in a five-game postseason series. The Texas black press called the series the "Negro National Baseball Championship."[59] Chicago won the series, three games to two, but there was none of the excitement and ceremony of the year before. No parades. No special rates from railroad companies for fans to attend. The *Houston Informer* published only one article, telling of Chicago's victory when the series ended, instead of providing game-by-game coverage.[60] The *Informer* itself experienced a major transformation in 1930, when editor Clifton Richardson was pushed out in favor of Carter G. Wesley. The transition in leadership further hurt the coverage of black baseball in Texas, as the *Informer* staff focused on in-house issues instead of events like baseball games.

The end of the 1930 season proved a dark time for African American baseball around the country, as well as in Texas. Rube Foster, founder of the Negro National League and the man who first brought national attention to black baseball in Texas, passed away. In Texas, Quincy Gilmore, founder and president of the TOL, resigned. The loss of these men foreshadowed the fate of professional black baseball in Texas.

J. B. Grigsby, former league vice president, took over the Texas-Louisiana League when Gilmore resigned. Grigsby optimistically announced that the upcoming baseball season would be "the most successful in the history of Texas baseball."[61] The league, though, consisted of only six teams, San Antonio, Galveston, Dallas, Shreveport, Houston, and New Orleans, as the 1931 season prepared to open.

Other black Texans attempted to build excitement about baseball in 1931. Julius White, a Houston nightclub owner and civil rights activist who also served as the president of Harris County's Negro Democratic Club, called for a parade on opening day in honor of the Black Buffaloes.[62] White said that since "Houston made a record for themselves in Texas . . . they deserve our attention and cooperation."[63]

The league added Monroe, Louisiana, and Fort Worth to its roster before the season began. Unfortunately, the optimism of people like White failed to be borne out. The economic situation of the country grew worse. For African Americans, cultural activities and social pursuits proved less important than finding jobs and providing for families. The Negro National League folded in March of 1932.[64] The Negro Southern League officially shut down later that year. The Negro League teams themselves either folded or followed the Homestead Grays' pattern of barnstorming, playing up to three games a day on weekends. In Texas, game attendance continued to dwindle.

San Antonio, under its new owner Cullen E. Taylor, attempted to make the team competitive by signing new players from around the country. The team brought in the Carter brothers, a first baseman and a shortstop, who formerly played in Memphis. San Antonio also signed Willie Williams, considered the best third baseman in the South, away from Atlanta of the Negro Southern League.[65]

Other teams also signed new players to strengthen themselves. The Fort Worth Black Cats recruited from the historically black colleges located in the state, signing several players from Bishop College and five from Wiley College. Unfortunately, the new athletes failed to change the team's play. In one three-game series, Fort Worth's new players committed fifteen errors.[66]

The Monroe team took the league championship in 1931, winning both halves of the season. Without a Texas team in first place, coverage of league games by the Texas black press almost disappeared. From opening day until the end of the campaign, the *Houston Informer* published exactly three articles on the baseball league. The *San Antonio Register* published no articles on the TL after the end of May. When the 1931 season ended, so did the Texas-Louisiana League.

The closing of the league marked the end of professional black baseball in Texas. Several semiprofessional leagues came and went after this, as did the professional Houston Eagles of the Negro American League, but none ever reached the level of the TOL. Its tenure was the high-water mark for African American baseball in Texas. During its three-year existence, the Texas-Oklahoma-Louisiana League reached near equality with the other black leagues in the country. It was a source of racial pride and community identity for black Texans. Its end foreshadowed the coming decline of black baseball in Texas and also showed the significant economic impact of the Great Depression on Texas and the country. However, the TOL bestowed a lasting reputation for African American baseball in Texas and left a permanent imprint on the Negro leagues and the game of baseball.

The Beginning of the End

THE DECLINE OF THE SEMIPROFESSIONAL GAME

6 The Texas-Oklahoma-Louisiana League gave black Texans their own professional baseball league and provided the Texas cities that hosted teams a community identity similar to large cities in the north with Negro League teams. Unfortunately, the TOL began competition at the start of the Great Depression. This ominous beginning was a preview of the problems all African American baseball would soon experience.

As the country's economic situation worsened, so did that of the TOL. The league closed down after the 1931 season. Over the next two decades interest in segregated baseball steadily decreased throughout the country. As African Americans faced new challenges brought by the Great Depression and World War II, baseball came to seem less important.

At the same time, the growing civil rights movement in the United States caused more African American fans to push for integration of white teams and leagues. When integration came, after World War II, the segregated teams lost almost all of their remaining support. Players like Jackie Robinson became the new symbol of African American community identity and racial pride. The professional Negro leagues and semiprofessional black teams were reminders of the past racial situation, while the integrated teams provided tangible examples of the success of civil rights.

For the semiprofessional teams, the impact of integration was immediate and devastating. Within a few years almost all of the once great clubs in Texas ceased to exist. The professional Negro leagues attempted to survive, but their demise soon followed.

The beginning of the end came with the Great Depression. Along with the closing of the TOL, the semiprofessional black teams in Texas also fell on hard times. In 1932, the Houston Black Buffaloes fielded a team of only ten players, in an attempt to keep down their payroll. J. M. Mitchell, the latest local African American businessman to own the Black Buffaloes, stated, "I mean to pay my men for service, and when they trot out on the field I want action and not alibis."[1] In San Antonio, the Black Indians' manager, Reuben Jones, quit after the team's first game and joined a club in Little Rock, Arkansas, for more money.[2] Compounding the problems faced by the Black Indians, the white San Antonio Indians lost their stadium to a fire and promptly appropriated the black team's park. Since the city of San Antonio owned the baseball park, the Black Indians were forced to comply. With the white team controlling the facility, the Black Indians played for more than a month on the road in 1932.[3] Problems such as this caused semiprofessional black baseball teams to collapse during the Depression. With the deepening economic crisis in the United States, fans worried more about providing for their families than attending baseball games or knowing where the Black Indians played their home games.

Even with the extra hardship as a result of the Depression, some semiprofessional black baseball teams continued to play. In Pittsburgh, the downturn hit the steel industry hard, and the play of semiprofessional baseball teams became a diversion from the hardships of daily life.[4] In Texas, the Austin Black Senators compiled a record of sixty wins, two losses, and two ties in 1932.[5] At the end of the season, they faced the Monroe Monarchs in a best-of-seven matchup that the black press dubbed the "Dixie Series."[6] Despite their impressive regular-season record, Austin lost to Monroe, four games to two. The success on the field of the Black Senators allowed them to attract more fans to games and hold on financially, while teams with a losing record tended to fold.

The economic problems faced by teams in Texas mirrored the economic problems of the Negro leagues and African American businesses throughout the country. It became too difficult for teams to participate in the Negro National League, and the league closed in 1931. The Negro Southern

League, a professional black minor league, closed in 1932.[7] The African American professional teams that survived, like the Kansas City Monarchs, made ends meet by barnstorming. The Monarchs faced all levels of competition. Newt Allen, a player on the team, remembered that Kansas City toured with the white House of David team for an entire year in order to draw crowds and share expenses. Then, in 1935, the Monarchs traveled to China, Japan, and the Philippines on a moneymaking tour.[8]

African American unemployment in Texas exceeded 8 percent by 1933. Black-owned businesses continued to fail. Only two black-owned banks, the Farmers' Bank and Trust in Fort Worth and the Farmers' Bank of Waco, were still operating by 1937.[9]

As the economic situation worsened, African American businessmen in Texas sought to form a new black baseball league in the state. On February 17, 1935, the organizers held a meeting at the Houston Black YMCA to determine if enough interest in a league existed. Led by Jim Liuzzo, an African American sports promoter from Houston, representatives from San Antonio, Beaumont, Lake Charles, and Houston all expressed interest. The men agreed to meet again on March 15 to begin the league's organization.[10]

At the meeting on March 15, the Negro Texas League officially began. With George C. Nelson, secretary of the Houston Black Buffaloes, presiding over the meeting, Houston, Galveston, Dallas, San Antonio, Austin, Beaumont, Tyler, and Waco all received franchises. The cities all had long-established African American baseball teams, as well as white Texas League stadiums. Furthermore, each city's population included a significant number of African Americans, from fifteen thousand to eighty thousand.[11]

The organizers elected officers and adopted a set of rules and regulations. Each team posted fifty dollars with the league treasurer as a good-faith deposit to protect against organizations dropping out midway through the season. Every club also promised to give 5 percent of its net receipts to the treasurer to cover day-to-day expenses. Finally, they created a pool of money to go to the top four finishers at the end of the season. According to the *Houston Informer*, the Negro Texas League offered "the only solution to attract and hold the interest of the Texas Negro baseball fans."[12]

Along with the creation of the new league, several professional black teams came to Texas on barnstorming tours. In March of 1935, the New York Black Yankees, Kansas City Monarchs, and Chicago American Giants all played, and defeated handily, the semiprofessional Negro Texas League members. The games drew large crowds, however. In a contest against a professional black baseball team, local teams and promoters could easily expect several hundred fans to attend, whereas when the local black semi-professional teams competed against each other, no one knew how many people might show up. The presence of players from Texas on the professional teams' rosters, such as Willie Wells, the star shortstop of the Chicago American Giants, also attracted fans.[13]

Unfortunately, the interest in teams such as the Monarchs failed to carry over to the Negro Texas League regular season. The fans never paid any real attention to the circuit. In the Texas cities hosting the black teams, African American incomes fell as unemployment rose.[14] Since tickets to the Negro Texas League's games cost fifty cents, more than a loaf of bread, fans chose not to spend their money on sports.

The low attendance for the Negro Texas League, as well as for the rest of semiprofessional black baseball in Texas, proved such a problem that a group identifying itself as "The League Boosters" wrote a letter to the editor of the *Houston Informer*, calling for more fans to attend.[15] In the article the Boosters attacked many of the excuses used by African Americans, such as the claim that the semiprofessional black teams played bad baseball and the teams needed new players with more ability. The Boosters responded that the only way for the clubs to acquire competent players would be if they made money. The only way the baseball teams made money was from gate receipts. Therefore, when fans attended regularly, the teams were able to sign the better players.[16]

The letter also presented a few questions to African American fans. The League Boosters challenged the racial pride and sense of community, asking, "Why do our people always try to drag their race down instead of trying to help them make good?"[17] According to the letter, "quite a few" black baseball fans regularly paid fifty cents a game to watch the local white squad.[18] If this attention, and money, went instead to black teams, then success was possible for the Negro Texas League, especially since segregation in the white minor league games in Texas relegated African Americans to a small section in the stadium farthest from home plate.

Despite the problems, the Negro Texas League officially began its season on May 11, 1935. Austin's mayor, Tom Miller, kicked off the season by throwing out the first pitch. The Austin Black Senators defeated the San

Antonio Black Missions by a score of 10 to 3. The game revealed some problems with the level of play and field conditions. San Antonio scored two of its runs on Austin errors in the fourth inning. After recording the second out of the inning, the Black Senators' first baseman, referred to only as Alexander in the newspaper, thought the inning over, threw the ball on the ground, and walked off the field, allowing a San Antonio base runner to score from second base. The other run-scoring error in the inning occurred when an Austin outfielder by the name of Lyons dropped a fly ball into a mud puddle and lost the ball, permitting the Black Missions' batter to record an inside-the-park home run. Despite these two miscues, Austin still tallied ten runs in the last three innings to win the game handily.[19]

The Black Senators and the Houston Black Buffaloes distinguished themselves early as the dominant powers in the league. Unfortunately, few fans came out to watch the teams. Sportswriters and team representatives pleaded for people to attend. One writer for the *Houston Informer* called baseball a "Texas institution, giving employment to some one hundred of the cream of the Negro athletes."[20] The crowds still failed to show up, for as Carlton Priestly and George Woods, black citizens of Lubbock during the Depression, explained, African Americans did not have "a lot of leisure time."[21] People spent a significant amount of their time working, looking for employment, or trying to take care of their family. With these priorities, attending baseball games seemed of little importance.[22] Also, the young men who participated in President Franklin Delano Roosevelt's New Deal programs, such as the Civilian Conservation Corps, found themselves removed from the cities to camps in rural areas. In these camps the men established their own softball teams and were less likely to travel to town to pay to watch a baseball game.

Participation in the New Deal programs brought some relief to African Americans, but the agencies mirrored the discrimination blacks faced elsewhere. The Texas black CCC camps, whose softball teams replaced semipro baseball as the main leisure activity for many African Americans, admitted only three hundred black males by the mid-1930s. Furthermore, less than half of African American farmers ever received aid through the Agricultural Adjustment Act.[23]

By June, the same sportswriters who less than a month before begged fans to attend Negro Texas League games began to criticize the teams' play. One article in the *Houston Informer* described Beaumont's performance to date, saying, "Beaumont started off like an old woman dancing, good but gave out early in the dance."[24] The league also suffered another major blow early on. League president George Nelson, also the Houston Black Buffaloes' secretary, quit his position because of the league's large financial losses and became a boxing promoter.[25] Nelson hoped to gain from the greater opportunity for African Americans in boxing, since the sport allowed integrated fights.

The members of the Negro Texas League resorted to stunts to attract fans. In the seventh inning of the first game of a doubleheader between Austin and Houston, Austin's catcher, "Pepper" Bassett, brought a rocking chair onto the field. With the help of a pitcher who had good control, Bassett proceeded to catch the remainder of the game without ever getting up from the chair.[26] The Galveston team owners took another approach. In mid-June they fired their manager and entire team, signing all new players and a new manager. Galveston's owners hoped that the change in personnel might spark some curiosity, as well as create a team that would win baseball games, leading to greater attendance.[27] Unfortunately, none of the publicity stunts provided long-term solutions, and attendance and fan interest remained low.

The league found itself unable to combat lack of interest and the Depression. On June 22, a headline in the *Houston Informer* read, "Lack of Attendance and Interest causes Negro Texas League to go on the Rocks."[28] Many of the teams in the league also closed their doors. The Dallas Black Giants and the Tyler Black Tigers played no more games until after World War II.[29]

Some teams persevered by scheduling games sporadically, continuing the practice of playing games only when a white stadium was available. Without other choices of facilities and playing times, the remaining black semiprofessional teams in Texas struggled. Teams such as the San Angelo Black Sheep Herders and Austin Black Senators found themselves forced to advertise in black newspapers to find competitors.[30]

Some of the better individual players moved onto professional African American teams for more money. "Pepper" Bassett, the catcher who played while sitting in a rocking chair, joined the Philadelphia Stars.[31] With Philadelphia, Bassett continued his stunt of catching in a rocking chair, which brought him national recognition.

Gus Greenlee, owner of the Pittsburgh Crawfords and founder of the second Negro National League in 1933, promoted Bassett's gimmick of catching in a rocking chair in order to attract fans. After signing Bassett in 1935, Greenlee had a special multicolored rocking chair built for use in nonleague games. The fans responded favorably to the stunt, but Bassett's ability as a player was enough to make him popular. In 1937, for example, he batted .444 and started in the East-West All-Star Game.[32] The black press in Texas reported on the success of Bassett and other local players, even though Texas teams floundered, providing heroes for black fans to follow and something to provide identity during the Depression.

In Mineola, the Texas Black Spiders held open tryouts to find players. The team also ran an advertisement in the paper calling for any squad interested in playing a game to contact its management.[33] Unfortunately, there are no records that tell what came of the tryouts or if any teams answered Mineola's offer for competition.

Other teams fared better. The Houston Black Buffaloes played the Kansas City Monarchs, Chicago American Giants, and Atlanta Black Crackers when the three professional black teams visited the Lone Star State on barnstorming tours. With the exception of these occasional exhibition games, Houston faced only teams of a lesser caliber, such as the Grand Prize Brewery.[34] A wide discrepancy in talent existed between the Black Buffaloes and their regular opponents during the late 1930s. For example, in one five-game period Black Buffalo pitchers struck out fifty-seven batters, an average of just under twelve per game.[35]

In an effort to survive, the Black Buffaloes took a cue from the professional African American teams and in 1936 undertook an eight-week barnstorming tour throughout the West and Canada. Along the way, they entered a national semiprofessional tournament for black teams in Wichita, Kansas.[36] The Black Buffaloes won the tournament handily, defeating Anthony, Kansas, 12 to 6; Emporia, 13 to 3; and Atchinson, 6 to 4.[37] Afterward, while playing in Canada, Houston compiled a record of sixteen wins and one loss.[38]

By the end of the 1930s, the Great Depression had claimed almost all of semiprofessional baseball in Texas, both black and white. Of the black semiprofessional teams, only a few survived in the harsh economic environment. The San Antonio Black Missions, formerly the Black Indians, stayed alive by playing teams like the All Stars of the Spanish American League, as well as teams from the Mexican leagues.[39] These games allowed the Black Missions to draw fans from San Antonio's large Hispanic population. Other teams, such as the Lubbock Black Hubbers, scheduled their games around major holidays, such as Juneteenth. Along with the celebration of the freedom of blacks in Texas, the game became a way for African Americans in Texas to celebrate their community and to relax from the daily pressures faced during the Depression. As a result, there was usually a large turnout for the individual games.[40]

Some teams resorted to showmanship and vaudeville-type acts. The Texas Black Spiders performed shadow ball, a slow-motion form of baseball pantomime, at every game.[41] In shadow ball, practiced by African American teams throughout the country, a team simulated a game without actually using a baseball. Pitchers pretended to pitch, batters pretended to bat, and fielders pretended to make amazing catches in the outfield and turn impressive double plays in the infield. The entire performance moved so smoothly and effortlessly that fans found it hard to believe a ball was not used.

Shadow ball proved a major form of cultural expression by the African American community, and pantomimed games became synonymous with black baseball. No evidence exists of white teams attempting a similar stunt. The level of grace and skill required for the players to convince the crowds that a real baseball was being used showed off African Americans' athletic ability.

For the more gifted players, not just in Texas but in all of the Negro leagues, the opportunity to change teams for a higher paycheck continued. William "Sug" Cornelius, a pitcher for the Chicago American Giants during the 1930s, recalled, "In the Depression years those salaries ran from $250 a month to $500 for really top players."[42] Willie Wells, the star shortstop from Austin, left his Negro League team on several occasions to play in Mexico for more money. A few other black Texans also left the country in order to play baseball, such as Pat Patterson who joined San Pedro de Macoris of the Dominican Republic.[43]

Overall, softball dominated black Texans' leisure time. Teams sponsored by the different Civilian Conservation Corp camps, and other New Deal agencies, played each other as a distraction from the Depression.[44] With these softball teams, black Texans tended to participate instead of watch. Softball continued to be an important pastime in America during World War II. The game required less skill at hitting and pitching, and thus allowed everyone an opportunity. Women also competed in growing numbers. As women entered jobs vacated by men who went off to fight in Europe and the Pacific, softball offered a means of relaxing after work, as well as dealing with fears for loved ones serving overseas. Young Japanese-American girls placed in the many American internment camps during the war turned to the game to soften the reality of their situation.[45] Participation in softball unified black men and women and reinforced baseball as a defining feature of the African American community.

Semiprofessional baseball in Texas changed drastically in 1941. After the Japanese bombed Pearl Harbor, the male population of Texas declined as the United States became involved in the war. With most of the eligible players either fighting in the war or playing a supporting role, the African American semiprofessional teams that had survived the Depression era closed down. Despite the loss of the teams, black baseball did not completely disappear. Teams from the different military camps played each other.[46] These camps and teams were segregated, but the all-black military units and their baseball teams still served as a source of pride for the black community. The camps' games allowed a form of escape from the pressure of military life and World War II.

As the war finally drew near a close, black Texans began to call for the return of baseball to the state. Unfortunately, as a part of wartime rationing, the Office of Defense Transportation placed limitations on the number of miles any team, white or black, could travel in a year. Buck Leonard, the Hall of Fame first baseman of the Homestead Grays, recalled, "During the war you couldn't go but 700 miles on the bus because of gasoline rationing."[47] This kept teams from barnstorming, making it next to impossible for them to make money. As a result, black Texans waited a little longer for the return of significant African American baseball. While they waited, sportswriters in Houston called for the city to place a team in the Negro Southern League.[48]

By the end of 1945, local black baseball had returned to Texas. An African American city league, in which local businesses sponsored teams, reemerged in Houston. J. Don Davis, a prominent local businessman, took charge of the league. Each team played one game a week, with a championship series at the end of the season. At the same time, the Houston Greyhounds, who began competing again in 1945, pushed for admittance into the professional-level Negro Southern League. The Southern League offered more stability because of the league's longer existence and connections with other professional Negro leagues. Some black Houstonians still hoped for the revival of the old Negro Texas League.[49]

A few African American teams, the Southwestern All-Stars, San Antonio Black Missions, and Dallas Green Monarchs, began to travel and play each other. The wartime restrictions still existed; these teams just limited the number of games they played so as to meet the ODT's regulations. The Dallas Green Monarchs even participated in the National Semiprofessional Tournament in Kansas City. Dallas played in the contest under the name Boeing Red Sox, because most of the players worked for the Boeing airplane plant in Dallas. The team won the tournament, beating the Walker AAF 4 to 3 in the championship game.[50] Despite the small number of African American teams after the war, black Texans who attended games witnessed some exciting baseball. In one game, Albert Overton, a pitcher for the Southwestern All-Stars, who formerly played for the Negro League Indianapolis Clowns, threw a no-hitter against the Fort Worth Black Giants.[51]

At the same time, the importance of baseball in the African American community continued because high-quality black baseball never completely left the state. The majority of the Negro National League and Negro American League teams, such as the Kansas City Monarchs, came to Texas to train in the preseason. Touring teams such as the Atlanta Black Crackers and Harlem Globetrotters, a baseball team named after the famous basketball squad, also faced each other in different cities around the state to the enjoyment of the Texas fans.[52] In October, Houston even hosted the 1945 North-South All-Star Game between the NNL and NAL, with such stars as Josh Gibson, James "Cool Papa" Bell, and Willie Wells participating.[53] These events and games reconnected black Texans to the national black community.

With 1945 and World War II ending without, for the most part, the revival of significant African American baseball in Texas, attention shifted to the 1946 season. Puss Ervin, a reporter for the Fort Worth black press, attempted to form a four-team semiprofessional black league. He hoped to include teams from Dallas, Fort Worth, Tulsa, and Oklahoma City. Ervin also wanted every team to play thirty to thirty-five games in a season and use local Texas League stadiums.[54] The proposed circuit never made it out of the planning stage. Meanwhile, city leagues, such as that in Houston, continued to play, featuring teams such as Houston Light and Power.[55] One team, the Texas Stars, even managed to tour the Midwest and Canada for three months.[56]

When Jackie Robinson joined the Brooklyn Dodgers in 1947, breaking the color barrier in the white major leagues, the entire country, and especially African Americans, became even more interested in major league baseball. African American attendance for Brooklyn's road games increased 21 percent, and the team's home attendance rose 400 percent as Americans, both black and white, turned out in record numbers to watch Robinson play.[57] The enthusiasm did not carry over to segregated baseball. The semi-professional black teams that remained in Texas played only sporadically and offered the fans less than stellar games. The occasional series between two traveling professional black teams, such as the Kansas City Monarchs and the Birmingham Black Barons who visited in 1947, proved the only opportunity for Texans to witness high-quality black baseball.[58]

Before Robinson, segregation led African Americans to focus on institutions within their own society as sources of identity. Now blacks could challenge racial stereotypes promoted by white teams and fans. African American players like Robinson excelled among their white teammates and opponents.

As attention in the black newspapers went to Jackie Robinson and not local teams, one Houston semiprofessional team, the Broadway Wolverines, went on an extensive road trip in 1947 in an effort to make some money. The tour lasted from May until August, with the team traveling throughout the Midwest and southern Canada. The Wolverines featured older players from Texas, such as pitcher Curley Andrews who had played in Houston for more than a decade. They also used young men from local black colleges, like shortstop Raymond Robinson of Samuel Huston College.[59]

With local city leagues as the main form of black baseball in Texas, African Americans focused most of their attention on major league baseball, especially integrated teams such as the Brooklyn Dodgers and Cleveland Indians. The shift in fan support was shown by an exhibition game in April of 1948, in which the Dodgers, with their African American stars Jackie Robinson and Roy Campanella, faced the Fort Worth Cats of the white Texas League. The Dodgers defeated their minor league affiliate easily, but spectators came from all over the state to watch the contest. Some railroads even chartered special cars to bring in fans who lived far from Fort Worth.[60]

More than eleven thousand people, half of whom were African Americans, attended.[61]

In contrast, black semiprofessional teams, such as the Houston Greyhounds, San Antonio Black Missions, and newly created Houston Black Aces, played the majority of their games on the road and out of state in an attempt to attract fans and draw enough revenue to survive.[62] Even the city leagues suffered. The Houston City League's membership dropped to four teams that played only on Sundays. Kelly's Drugs, Weingarten, Foley Brothers, and Southern Acid all saw their season shortened, lasting from June until early August.[63] The Dallas Black Giants began competing again only in 1948, more than a decade after they shut down.[64]

The late 1940s proved a tenuous time for African American baseball around the country. With the success of Jackie Robinson and Larry Doby, major league teams signed away the best players from the professional black teams, as well as from semiprofessional and college squads. Without their stars, the quality of play in African American baseball dropped off precipitously. As a result, fans chose to attend the games of integrated major league teams that exhibited superior play. It was through these integrated teams that the black community found its identity and cultural expression. Black baseball suffered severely in the late 1940s and early 1950s, as was evident when the Negro National League disbanded after the 1948 season.

In a last-ditch effort to survive, the Negro American League recognized the permanence of integration in major league baseball and sought to set up teams in the large southern cities that were still segregated. The Negro American League officials hoped that with the southern minor leagues refusing to sign African Americans, the black communities in these cities retained enough interest in African American baseball to support an all-black team. As a result, professional black baseball returned to Texas in 1949 with the creation of the Houston Eagles of the Negro American League.

At the same time, local team owners in Texas made one final attempt to revive semiprofessional black baseball in the state with the creation of a new Negro Texas League. In January of 1949, the owners of the larger African American teams met in Fort Worth to outline the league's operating procedures and officers. Ten cities received franchises: Dallas, Fort Worth, Marshall, Longview, Austin, Shreveport, Tyler, New Orleans, Waco, and Monroe. These cities had a tradition of black baseball, and most of them had white Texas League stadiums where games could take place.

The Negro Texas League also recognized that white teams were searching every level of black baseball for players with the ability to play in the major leagues. As a result, the Negro Texas League came to an agreement with Major League Baseball that gave any black player in Texas whose skills distinguished him on the field a chance to try out for the recently integrated professional teams.[65] Two weeks after the leagues reached the agreement, Samuel Haynes, a former star player at Prairie View A&M University, received a tryout with the Brooklyn Dodgers.[66]

The Negro Texas League offered an exciting brand of baseball, which in the past would have received significant support from the black community. The skills exhibited by the players paled in comparison to those of players in the white minor leagues in the state, or of the Houston Eagles of the Negro American League. The Negro Texas League teams took their players from the local community, while the minor leagues and Houston Eagles consisted of more competent players from all over the country. But even though the Negro Texas League was not the highest level of the sport, spectators usually saw high-scoring, offensive-oriented contests. In one slugfest between the Dallas Black Giants and the Kerrville All-Stars, which the Black Giants won 14 to 13, Dallas's center fielder, Raymond Lott, hit for the cycle. He had five hits in five at-bats in the game: a single, a double, a triple, and two home runs.[67] Even with offensive feats like Lott's, fan attendance remained low, forcing teams to take out advertisements in the newspapers to find opponents outside of the league in an effort to make money. Furthermore, despite integration at the national level, in Texas black teams still found themselves unable to compete against whites.

Yet baseball fans did not completely shun African American semiprofessional baseball during the late 1940s. Occasionally large crowds turned out to watch two black teams compete. For one game in Kerrville, two thousand fans came out to see Dallas defeat the Kerrville All-Stars. The Black Giants won in eleven innings. The African American press tried to boost the game, saying the fastball of Dallas's starting pitcher, manager Bill Blair, "blazed by the batters with the speed of a jet."[68]

Semiprofessional African American baseball also offered exciting and colorful players and events for the fans that attended the games. Ruben Samuel recalled his playing days in the late 1940s: "Back in them days I use to eat peanut patties. . . . I was stealing second base and my peanut patty fell, fell out. I was safe and I went back and got my peanut patty and I got thrown out of the game. Boy them boys carried me about that. . . . Every time I hit a home run they would give me a peanut patty."[69] By the end of May, the Negro Texas League's membership was much different from that announced at the original meeting. Only six teams remained in the league: Amarillo, Kerrville, Dallas, Fort Worth, San Antonio, and Shreveport. The other members all closed down, unable to stay afloat. At the same time, almost twenty African Americans appeared on the rosters of major league teams. With the success of players like pitcher Don Newcombe, who won Rookie of the Year honors in 1949 as he led the Brooklyn Dodgers to the National League pennant, more white teams signed black players and more African American fans turned their attention to integrated teams.

Meanwhile, semiprofessional black baseball in Texas struggled to survive. Of the teams remaining in the Negro Texas League, the Dallas Black Giants and the Fort Worth All-Nations stood tied for first place. In an effort to attract as many fans as possible, no matter what ethnicity, the Fort Worth All-Nations fielded a team made up of African Americans, whites, Hispanics, and Cubans. The approach failed to attract fans, as well as causing black Texans to view the team as not representative of their community.

Rumors also circulated through the black press that major league scouts attended Dallas's games to get a look at the Black Giants' star shortstop, seventeen-year-old Ernie Banks. Fans went to check out Banks and to spot the major league scouts in the stands. Banks provided a counterpoint for the image offered by the All-Nations.[70]

In June, Dallas and Fort Worth faced each other for sole possession of first place in the Negro Texas League. Because of the proximity and rivalry between the two cities, several hundred fans attended the game. Led by shortstop Banks, who got three hits in four at-bats in the game, the Black Giants defeated the All-Nations to take a one-game lead in the league standings.[71]

With the exception of games like the ones between Dallas and Fort Worth, overall league attendance remained extremely low. As fans turned their attention to the accomplishments of African American baseball players in the major leagues, such as Larry Doby and Jackie Robinson, the black press accommodated them by covering the big leaguers' actions, pushing the local teams from the sports page. In Dallas, Black Giants' manager James McCray, hoping to raise attendance, announced that he planned to feature his star local players, specifically shortstop Ernie Banks and center fielder Raymond Lott, more in team games.[72]

Unfortunately, no change could bring in enough fans and money to save the league. On July 22, 1949, the Negro Texas League officially closed, this time for good. Along with the league, every one of its teams, except the New Orleans Creoles, who continued for a few more years as a touring team, ceased operations.[73]

In 1950 rumors circulated in the black press that an unnamed source wanted to form a new semiprofessional league, known as the Texas and Louisiana Negro Baseball League. Unfortunately, the plans never amounted to anything more than talk and speculation. The loss of the Negro Texas League and the teams that made up its membership marked the end of organized semiprofessional African American baseball in Texas. A few teams continued to play locally into the 1950s, but the long tradition and history of semiprofessional black baseball in Texas disappeared. The integration of the southern minor leagues, led by the Texas League in 1952 with pitcher Dave Hoskins of the Dallas Giants, signaled the end of segregated baseball.[74] Community teams also closed down in 1950. In Diboll, the Dragons folded after the manager stole three hundred dollars from the team. The loss of the team caused most of the African American players in Diboll to quit baseball altogether.[75] By 1950, the Houston Eagles of the Negro American League were all that remained of African American professional baseball in Texas, and they moved to New Orleans in 1951.

Throughout the first half of the twentieth century, "local fellows" on teams like the Lubbock Black Hubbers had played once a week, with teams making just enough to cover expenses.[76] All of the players worked full-time jobs to provide for themselves and their families. Even though the players might occasionally "pass the hat" or get a share of the gate profits at games, they received no salary from the team and thus fell under the amateur or club team heading. Some men, like George Forkerway of the Abilene Black Eagles, competed for the local team while attending high school.[77] Played strictly for the enjoyment of the game, black semiprofessional baseball served as the foundation for all of African American baseball in Texas, making the teams an important feature of the black community and the most prevalent image of African American masculinity. Strength and security lay in community, and local baseball games were a community affair.[78]

The Houston Eagles and the
End of Negro League Baseball

7 While Texas played a major role in the growth and development of the Negro leagues and the game of baseball, black Texans also were a part of the end of independent African American baseball. By the close of the 1940s, black semiprofessional baseball teams, still suffering from the impact of the Great Depression and World War II, had steadily disappeared from the Texas landscape. At the same time, the integration of Major League Baseball created a powerful new opponent for segregated teams and leagues. African American baseball fans began to look to integrated teams and black players on these teams as sources of community identity. Texas's role in these events began in 1949 when African American professional baseball returned to the state in the form of the Houston Eagles of the Negro American League (NAL). The arrival of the Eagles came as a dying effort of black baseball to compete with the integrated major leagues. That Texas played a role at the end of African American baseball was fitting considering the importance of the state and its black citizens in the creation of the first Negro League by Rube Foster and the rise of the sport to prominence through the Texas-Oklahoma-Louisiana League and such players as Willie Wells. The Eagles offered closure for this legacy.

After World War II, baseball experienced a massive increase in popularity. White major league players, such as Ted Williams and Joe DiMaggio, who had taken time off to fight for America, returned to the sport. Over 90 percent of major league baseball players served in the military during World War II. With the influx of these players, military baseball provided enjoyment and a sense of camaraderie for the U.S. soldiers who played the game wherever they were stationed.[1] The importance of baseball to the soldiers during the war led fans to attend games in record numbers once the conflict ended.

After the war, some black players returned from the armed forces, such as Max Manning of the Newark Eagles, while others, like Willie Wells, who played in Mexico during the war years, also returned. But the excitement over baseball in the military failed to extend to African Americans. For African American soldiers, boxing, which was integrated, proved highly attractive. Boxing champs Sugar Ray Robinson and Joe Louis put on exhibition bouts against white competitors in front of large, integrated crowds while a part of the army.[2] In contrast, military baseball teams remained segregated. The large military bases, such as the Great Lakes Naval Training Station, only allowed African Americans to play against each other. Jackie Robinson, who was already nationally known from his days as an athlete at the University of California, Los Angeles, found himself not allowed to compete for the Fort Riley team in Kansas where he was stationed.[3]

Still, the national excitement and patriotism following the U.S. victory in World War II made baseball highly profitable in the late 1940s. Black baseball in Texas got caught up in the postwar excitement over the revival of sports. African Americans felt proud of the role they had played in the Allied victory over Hitler and his racist ideology. The participation by black soldiers on the battlefield and black workers in defense industry jobs led many African Americans to look for integration into American society.

During the war, many of Texas's black semiprofessional teams closed down as players and fans joined the war effort. African American baseball never completely left the state, though. Throughout the early 1940s, many of the professional black teams came through Texas on barnstorming tours. In 1945, the Negro National League and Negro American League held a North-South All-Star Game in Houston, featuring such stars as Josh Gibson, "Cool Papa" Bell, and Roy Campanella.[4]

With the end of the war, African Americans in Texas began to push for greater opportunities and access. Following the Supreme Court case of *Smith v. Allright* in 1944 that overturned the "white only" political primaries in Texas, African American voting increased in the state. By the late 1940s, over 18 percent were registered to vote, more than in any other southern state.[5]

In this environment of increased political and social involvement, fans in Texas began calling for the return of black professional baseball. One sportswriter for the *Houston Informer* declared that since Houston possessed "the largest black population in the South according to ratio," it stood to reason that there was one person in the city with the ability and experience to organize a successful black professional baseball team.[6] According to the reporter, the once prominent Houston Black Buffaloes failed because of limited public support and inexperience by the team owners in financial matters.[7] Following his logic, if a knowledgeable, competent person organized a black team, it would be a success.

All of baseball, black and white, changed in 1947 when, on April 15, Jackie Robinson, a former All-American athlete at UCLA and an African American, played for the Brooklyn Dodgers against the Boston Braves. Robinson achieved considerable professional success after integrating Major League Baseball, leading the Dodgers to numerous National League pennants and one World Series championship. He won the Rookie of the Year award in 1947, as well as the Most Valuable Player award in 1951. According to historian William Simons, "The integration of baseball was the most widely commented on episode in American race relations at the time."[8]

Robinson's reintegration of the major leagues was the culmination of years of hard work by many different groups. Wendell Smith, the sports editor for the *Pittsburgh Courier*, one of the largest African American newspapers in the country, carried out a twelve-year campaign for the integration of baseball. He published articles and editorials about black players and the lunacy of the racial situation in the game. Smith even recommended Robinson to Branch Rickey, the president of the Dodgers, less than a month before Rickey signed Robinson in 1945.[9]

Another person who campaigned for the integration of baseball was Lester Rodney. Rodney served as sports editor for the *Daily Worker*, the national paper for the American Communist Party. The *Daily Worker*'s circulation was not as large as that of major papers like the *New York Times*, but it still constituted a significant, and extremely vocal, voice for integration. Beginning in 1936, Rodney used his newspaper as a forum to campaign for the integration of baseball. While not as influential as Smith, mainly because of his paper's political creed, Rodney helped illustrate the hypocrisy of the racial segregation in the sport and the country when the United States officially professed itself as the nation of democracy, freedom, and equality, but kept some of the best players out of the national pastime simply because of the color of their skin.[10]

Robinson's accomplishments on the field also brought another argument against segregation, the financial success of his team. The Dodgers saw their home attendance figures increase by 400 percent in 1947 alone. This increase was due in a large part to the number of African American fans that flocked to games. Attendance figures for Dodgers road games also skyrocketed as black fans turned out in large numbers for every game to watch Robinson.[11]

When Robinson broke the color barrier in Major League Baseball, he paved the way for every black player that followed. Larry Doby of the Newark Eagles joined the Cleveland Indians later in the 1947 season. The next year, more African Americans entered the major leagues and excelled. After Robinson, Don Newcombe also won the Rookie of the Year award. Roy Campanella, the former student of Biz Mackey, won three National League Most Valuable Player awards while with the Dodgers.

The success of these athletes in integrated baseball also affected the way the African American community defined itself. During the first half of the twentieth century, blacks throughout Texas and the country looked to institutions within their own communities as sources of racial pride and identity. With the system of racial segregation in the United States denying African Americans access to almost all aspects of white society, all-black businesses, schools, churches, social organizations, and sports teams served as significant cultural entities outside the control of whites. With integration, this cultural identity changed. The change occurred gradually in many cases, such as with schools, but nonetheless African Americans sought inclusion into the broader American culture and society. The success of black players on white teams provided a new model for black masculinity. African Americans now had tangible evidence of their physical and intellectual equality with, and in some cases superiority to, whites. As a result, the older institutions suffered. However, organizations like the U.S. Army that also served as sources of black pride and consciousness were still segregated. Through the sport's early integration, baseball, as the "national pastime," surpassed the army. Desegregation of other institutions like the military would add to African American racial pride and consciousness, but only after baseball blazed the trail.

With the success of African American players in the majors, segregated black baseball went into decline. Fans preferred to attend the games of the integrated professional teams. When the Brooklyn Dodgers played the Fort Worth Cats, a member of the white Texas League, in a spring training game, more than eleven thousand fans, half of whom were black, came from all over the state to watch.[12] As fan support shifted away from African American baseball, so did press coverage. The black newspapers daily published the exploits of African Americans in the major leagues, while ignoring all-black teams.

The Negro League owners and players recognized the imminent loss of their most talented athletes to integrated baseball. Some owners sought financial compensation from major league teams that signed away black players. Unfortunately for Negro League owners, their own legacy of players jumping contracts and teams signing away players without any consequences left black teams without a legal basis for compensation.[13]

The Cleveland Buckeyes of the Negro American League attempted to improve their financial situation by copying the major leagues and signed Eddie Klep in 1946 as the first white player in the Negro leagues. Unlike when Robinson joined Brooklyn, there was no press conference when Klep signed. Cleveland's "white" newspaper even ignored the event. Klep, well past his prime and just trying to extend his career, was released by the team during its preseason. He proved not talented enough to make the team, but he also faced resentment from blacks who did not want him on their club.[14]

In other efforts to compete with the changing scene, the commissioners of the Negro National League and the Negro American League, Tom Wilson and J. B. Martin, attempted to save African American baseball by getting the two leagues incorporated into Major League Baseball as minor leagues. This action would have secured contracts with players, guaranteed financial compensation for signed-off players, and brought outside financial help to struggling black teams. Because of the Negro leagues' long history with gamblers, and the white owners' fear of gambling following the 1919 White Sox scandal, Happy Chandler, the commissioner of Major League Baseball, refused the request.[15]

The loss of their best players and fans, as well as loss of coverage by black newspapers, proved to be the death blow for African American baseball teams. The Newark Eagles saw their yearly attendance drop from one hundred and twenty thousand in 1946 to fifty-seven thousand in 1948. Also in 1948, the Negro National League, no longer able to compete economically, closed down permanently, taking with it many of its teams.[16]

As professional black baseball struggled to stay alive, the Negro American League incorporated some of the teams from the Negro National League, making one big league divided into two divisions. Tired of losing money, Effa and Abe Manley, the owners of the Newark Eagles, sold their club after the 1948 season to William H. Young, a native Texan who became a prominent Memphis dentist.[17] Young decided to move his franchise to Houston, hoping to capitalize on the city's large African American population, more than eighty thousand people, as well as the lack of major league competition.[18]

The new Houston Eagles joined the Western Division of the Negro American League. The NAL made other decisions to cut down on expenses, such as playing only on weekends, which helped keep salaries down. The Eagles also decided to play all of their home games at night in order to attract more fans.[19] Unfortunately, the Eagles failed to make an impact in the NAL. The team worked out for spring training in Hot Springs, Arkansas, and from the very beginning experienced problems. Pitcher Max Manning failed to report to camp, holding out for more money. The team's two best players, pitcher Leon Day and third baseman Ray Dandridge, also refused to join the team, prompting the new owners to sell both players.[20]

The Eagles' bad luck continued as they lost their opening series of the campaign. They dropped both games of a doubleheader to the Birmingham Black Barons by scores of 4 to 1 and 4 to 3. Playing on a muddy field in Birmingham, the Eagles gave the series away by committing numerous errors.[21] After their loss to the Black Barons, the Eagles returned to Houston for their home opener against the Memphis Red Sox. Despite the team's early problems, baseball fever swept through Houston. Older African American baseball fans had longed for a professional black team in Houston since the demise of the TOL in 1931. The *Houston Informer* proclaimed the city as "one of the greatest Negro League baseball towns in the country."[22] According to the paper, this enthusiastic interest for baseball came from the large number of people from small and rural towns who had moved to Houston during the Great Depression and World War II.

For these fans, baseball gained its place in America as the national pastime by being a "clean sport" that "affords recreation for folk in all walks of life, from the most menial and common of laborers to the highest professionals."[23] These fans previously identified with local semiprofessional teams that represented the community. The promoters of the Eagles hoped their team would establish itself in the same role within the black community in Houston.

Another selling point that excited fans about the Eagles' home opener turned out to be the Memphis manager, Texan Willie Wells. Wells no longer had the skills he exhibited as a youth playing in Austin, but his name still had strong drawing power. Also, Wells's son, Willie Wells, Jr., played shortstop for the Red Sox, while Wells, Sr., played second base. The chance to see the first father and son to play on the same team at the same time in baseball history attracted many fans.[24]

Managed by Reuben Jones, the Eagles fielded such players as Bob Harvey and Johnnie Davis, two of the best hitters in the league. Manager Jones called shortstop "Curly" Williams the next Jackie Robinson, while catcher Leon Ruffin had played in the league longer than any other current catcher.[25] Unfortunately, the citizens of Houston knew none of these players. As a result, once the initial excitement subsided, the Eagles struggled throughout their two-year existence to field teams that the fans knew and wanted to watch. When the Eagles fielded local players, the African American community found it easy to rally around and identify with the team, win or lose. Without local players, it was more difficult to find support among black Texans, especially since the squad was not competitive in the league.

At the same time, a growing civil rights movement in Texas sought to integrate society. In 1949, the local NAACP chapter in Houston pressured the city to integrate the public library.[26] Beginning in 1946 and lasting until the Supreme Court returned a decision in 1950, Herman Sweatt, an African American, fought to integrate the University of Texas Law School.[27] With an ever-increasing number of black Texans focusing their attention on civil rights issues, segregated baseball went directly against the growing interest in equal access.

Still, the opening of a new team and baseball season garnered some excitement in Houston. The Eagles' home opener against the Memphis Red Sox was played at Buffalo Stadium, the white Texas League park. Dr. John Davis, a local black doctor named "Man of the Year" by the *Houston Informer*, threw out the first pitch, and Roscoe Cavitt, executive secretary of the Chamber of Commerce, gave a speech.[28] The pregame excitement carried over into the game. With two outs and runners on second and third, the Eagles attempted a double steal. Jimmy Wilkes, the Eagles' runner on second, got caught in a rundown and was tagged out. An argument soon arose between an unnamed Red Sox player and an umpire known only as "Roughhouse" over whether the Red Sox tagged Wilkes out before Andrew Patterson, the man on third, crossed home plate.[29] The umpire resolved the situation by ejecting the Red Sox player from the game and giving the run to Houston. Unfortunately, Houston scored no more runs in the game, losing 6 to 1.

The next weekend, May 15 and 16, the Eagles won their first league series, defeating the Kansas City Monarchs two games to one. After dropping the first game, Houston came back to win the second and third games. In the bottom of the eighth inning in the second game, Eagles outfielder Johnny Davis hit a home run to win the game 2 to 0. In the third game, Davis hit another home run, and Johnny Williams scored the winning run in the seventh inning. The victory led the *Houston Informer* to declare, "The Eagles are definitely on the rise for pennant contention."[30]

The Eagles lineup became more formidable as the season went on, when their ace pitcher, Max Manning, finally signed his contract and reported to the team. The twenty-nine-year-old right-hander had posted a record of nineteen wins and three losses in 1946. The team also added Curley Andrews, a veteran infielder from Houston, in an attempt to attract fans by using local players.[31]

Despite the changes, Houston had only a .500 winning percentage by the middle of June and stood next to last in the Western Division.[32] Also, the public still knew next to nothing about the Eagles. The team executives assumed the fans knew the Eagles' history in New Jersey, as well as the team's former players, Larry Doby, Don Newcombe, and Monte Irvin, who now played in the major leagues. The *Houston Informer* reported that citizens still asked, "Are the Eagles a semi-pro outfit?" and "Why aren't more local players on the team?"[33] Not helping matters, the Eagles experienced a scheduling conflict that prevented them from using the white stadium in Houston. As a result, the team went on a multiweek road trip that kept the fans from learning about the team.[34] Furthermore, the club failed to attract fans from outside the city. In the past, the African American communities throughout the state looked to the black teams as a source of cultural identity.

Now, fans in places such as Dallas or Abilene paid little or no attention.

The Eagles still experienced some bright spots in their season. Williams stood in fourth place in the NAL batting race with an average of .364.[35] On June 18 and 19, the team swept a series against the Cleveland Buckeyes. In the seventh inning of the first game, Boo Wilson hit an inside-the-park home run for the Eagles. Johnny Davis also hit a home run completely out of the park, while at the same time pitching a complete-game shutout to win 4 to 0.[36]

Beginning on June 26, the Eagles and the Chicago American Giants faced each other in a six-game series. They played in Chicago for the majority of the games, but also played in other cities across Illinois in an effort to draw more fans who might not travel to Chicago. The Eagles counted on the bat of their first baseman, Johnny Williams, to carry the team.[37] Unfortunately, Houston lost the series five games to one.[38] Around the same time, the team began to hurt financially because of low attendance. In response, team owner W. H. Young attempted to make some money by selling pitcher Jonas Gaines's contract to fellow Negro League team the Philadelphia Stars.[39]

Once the team returned home, the Eagles' owner and team management attempted to change their luck, as well as increase attendance, by holding an Eagles appreciation day. Centered on a doubleheader against the Philadelphia Stars, the Eagles sponsored a parade, hired a band to play music between innings, and gave out prizes to the fans. The players also received gifts from city representatives.[40] The goal of the promotion was to establish a community identity with the team based on a cultural celebration. The organizers hoped this would supersede whether or not the team won or lost. In the end, none of these efforts changed the outcome. The Eagles lost their series against Philadelphia and the fans still failed to attend in large numbers. With the loss, the *Houston Informer* became more pessimistic about the team. The paper placed blame for the loss on the players. A statement by the *Informer*'s sports reporter illustrated the level of frustration felt by the fans in Houston: "Johnny Davis's bat has wilted. Of all things Tuesday night, he had the audacity to strike out when he knows his public expects him to knock one over the left field fence every time he comes to bat."[41]

The Eagles finished the first half of the 1949 season in last place. Manager Reuben Jones retired at the break, citing old age.[42] Hoping to improve in the second half, Houston hired Roy "Red" Parnell, former player-manager of the Houston Black Buffaloes, as the new manager. The Eagles also pointed to Johnny Davis, their right fielder who led the NAL in home runs, as a bright spot.

Unfortunately, the second half of the 1949 season proved no different from the first. Houston continued to lose, standing firmly in last place in its division. The accomplishments of black major league players like Larry Doby and Don Newcombe received more attention in the state's black newspapers. African Americans now looked to the stars of integrated baseball as sources of racial pride and cultural identity. As the 1949 season came to a close, Houston fired manager Red Parnell and promoted catcher Leon Ruffin to interim manager. In an effort to end the season on a positive note, Ruffin revamped his lineup, playing players who exhibited a "will to win."[43] None of the moves made any difference; the Eagles still lost most of their games.

The Negro American League and the Houston Eagles failed to turn a profit during the 1949 season. Every team in the league saw its attendance decline. In Chicago, the American Giants, once the most profitable team in black baseball, averaged only three thousand fans a game, while playing all their home games in forty-eight-thousand-seat Comiskey Park.[44] Even the annual East-West All-Star game ceased to be a success. Jimmie Blair, a writer for the Associated Negro Press, attributed the problem to the fact that the major leagues signed the best black players through extensive scouting and holding tryout camps. For black baseball to survive, he believed, it needed to follow Major League Baseball's example.[45]

Effa Manley, former owner of the Newark Eagles, issued her own statement to the Associated Negro Press about the situation of African American baseball. She said that unless black teams attracted fans, the Negro leagues might disappear completely. The burden fell on the press to promote black games. She also believed that African American teams needed to foster better play in order to keep fans interested.[46]

Following the 1949 season, some people still had positive words about the Eagles. Chick Solomon, an old-time black baseball player who lived in Houston and called himself a student of the game, declared Eagles outfielder Jimmy Wilkes the "best defensive center fielder in baseball today."[47] Not just in black baseball, he said, but in "baseball period."[48] Solomon's opinion did not mean much to the African American community, which continued to wholeheartedly support integrated baseball.

As the Baltimore Elite Giants and Chicago American Giants faced each other in the Negro World Series, last-place Houston played its own post-season game against the New Orleans Creoles, failing to attract much attention. The main selling point of the Houston and New Orleans game was not the two teams' play, but the Creoles' female second baseman, Toni Stone.[49]

Further proof of the shift of black fan support came following the 1949 season when Jackie Robinson took an all-star team of black major and minor leaguers on a barnstorming tour of the country. Accompanied by Larry Doby, Roy Campanella, and Don Newcombe, Robinson's team faced a team of all-stars from the Negro American League.[50] While the Houston Eagles drew only a few hundred fans to their games, several thousand fans packed the Eagles stadium when the all-star teams played in town. The spectators sat through the cold and rain to cheer Robinson's team onto a 6 to 2 win.[51]

Fighting to survive, the NAL held a two-day meeting in Chicago in February of 1950 to make plans for the upcoming season. According to rumors, the league wanted to remove the Philadelphia Stars, Baltimore Elite Giants, and New York Cubans because of the teams' poor play and low gate receipts. Owners in the Western Division felt dissatisfied with a ten-team league and saw the removal of the three Eastern teams as the easiest solution. When the idea came to a vote, it failed but showed the uneasiness in the NAL.[52]

Some changes were made at the meeting. The team representatives approved a switch in ownership for the Memphis Red Sox. The league members voted out Dr. W. S. Martin, owner of the franchise since 1928. Martin's brother, Dr. B. B. Martin, received the club, but W. S. Martin maintained ownership of the team's home in Memphis, Martin Stadium, as well as the copyright to the team name.[53]

The Houston Eagles made some changes of their own. Team owner Young brought Red Parnell back as manager, while interim manager Leon Ruffin returned to playing catcher. Houston also sold its best pitcher, Rufus Lewis, to the Brooklyn Dodgers and brought in Bob Turner, recently released by the Boston Braves, to serve as an assistant coach and catcher.

To fill Lewis's spot, the Eagles signed eighteen-year-old left-handed pitcher John Wesley Odell.[54] The team also held an open tryout on March 25, to attract good local players who might give the Eagles a strong local appeal.[55]

Houston prepared for its season opener against the Chicago American Giants on April 15 with much fanfare in the local black press, hoping to build excitement for the upcoming season. Manager Parnell declared the team in excellent shape and ready to bring home the pennant.[56] According to the *Houston Informer*, the only problem the team faced was keeping the "big league and white minor" teams from raiding the Eagles' players.[57] Parnell boasted that he "wasn't planning to drop any games this season, least of all his opening game."[58] He went on to add: "I want to put Houston back on the baseball map again. And with the type of youngsters and seasoned veterans I have this year, I don't believe we'll be anybody's pushover. . . . I promise Houston fans that if they'll give me their support, they'll get a team they can be proud of."[59]

As the season began, the Eagles looked like they might live up to Parnell's lofty predictions. Playing in Galveston instead of Houston, in order to take advantage of the island city's large stadium, the Eagles defeated the American Giants 15 to 9 in the opening game. In the sixth inning, Houston sent a total of twelve men to the plate and scored nine runs. Unfortunately, only five hundred people came out, leaving several thousand seats empty.[60]

On May 14, the Eagles returned to Houston for their first home series of the season against the Cleveland Buckeyes, which the Eagles won two games to one. To kick off the series, Houston Mayor Oscar F. Holcombe threw out the first pitch and a Marine Corps unit performed drills in a pregame ceremony. Rufus Lewis, the pitcher whose contract the Eagles sold to the Brooklyn Dodgers, returned to Houston after failing to make the team and pitched the first game of the day/night doubleheader.[61] After the series, Manager Parnell issued a challenge to the Houston fans, saying, "The boys are hustling to display wares that will mean a trip upstairs, but the fans must turn out and help maintain a proving ground for these future stars. I am sure they won't let their youth down."[62] Parnell's plea to the community proved significant for other reasons. By stating that the players wanted to move "upstairs," Parnell admitted the dominant place of integrated baseball in the African American community. The Eagles and all of Negro League baseball now only served as possible stepping-stones.

There were other ominous signs of the league's economic situation and diminishing level of cultural importance. Owner Young admitted in the *Houston Informer* that he suffered heavy financial losses in 1949.[63] But he spoke with confidence: "We had some things to straighten out. All is well as we open up the year and I know the citizens of Houston will give their own manager Red Parnell a welcome return to his home by good attendance of the games played by a team that we spent plenty on to make Houston proud of."[64]

Other teams in the Negro American League experienced the same problems. Every team played before small crowds. In Chicago, only two thousand fans came out to watch the Chicago American Giants face Houston in Comiskey Park, while across town on the same day, forty thousand people saw the New York Giants with Hank Thompson, formerly of the Kansas City Monarchs, defeat the Chicago Cubs. In New York, the same scenario took place. Six thousand spectators came to the Polo Grounds to watch the New York Cubans play the Indianapolis Clowns, while fifty-four thousand people witnessed a game between the New York Yankees and Cleveland Indians, the latter led by former Negro League stars Larry Doby and Satchel Paige.[65]

With team optimism high after the club's victory over Cleveland, the Eagles prepared to face the Birmingham Black Barons. Unfortunately, rumors started circulating throughout Houston that the Eagles planned to return to their previous home in Newark, New Jersey. Newark's franchise in the white International League moved to Springfield, leaving the town without a team. With the Eagles experiencing financial difficulty in Houston, the city of Newark invited the team to return. Team owner Young turned down the offer, however, and gave Eagles supporters assurances that the team liked Houston and planned to stay.[66] Still, fans were wary, and this apprehension was reflected in attendance figures.

Problems continued to arise for the entire Negro American League. Bill Cash, a veteran catcher for the Philadelphia Stars, left his team to play in Mexico. Promised more money, Cash followed four other Stars players, all pitchers, south of the border.[67]

The Eagles, the preseason pick to win the Western Division, began to play better baseball in 1950 than the year before. Near the end of the first half of the season, they found themselves in third place in their division, a step up from last place the previous season. Despite their improved play, only small crowds came out.[68] When the first half ended, few people in Houston noticed that the Indianapolis Clowns and Kansas City Monarchs won the two Negro American League divisions.

In the *Houston Informer*, major league news continued to dominate the sports page. In fact, the paper covered the local black softball league more than it covered the Eagles. The exploits of such teams as the Grand Prize Pale Drys and the Houston Cotton Clubbers appeared every week in the paper, while the Eagles received mention only monthly. Why this was so remains a mystery. Perhaps it was because the softball teams consisted of local citizens, while the Eagles players were still mostly unknown and had compiled a less than stellar record.

Every other team in the league experienced the same problems. In an effort to survive, the NAL tried different means to attract fans. In Chicago, the American Giants attempted to compete with the Cubs and White Sox by signing two white players, Lou Chirban, a pitcher, and Louis Clarizion, an outfielder. William Little, the owner of the American Giants, called the players' signing an "experiment."[69] Since the white major league teams increased their attendance by signing black players, Little hoped to attract more white fans.[70] Unfortunately, his idea never caught on in the Negro American League and failed to change the financial situation, the same result as when Cleveland signed Eddie Klep a few years before.

Houston, which started the season playing well, began to drop rapidly in the standings. By the middle of July, the Eagles' record stood at seventeen wins and nineteen losses, placing them fourth in the Western Division.[71] After the Eagles started the second half of the season by losing their first five games, the *Houston Informer* published no articles on them until the East-West All-Star game at the end of August. Instead, the paper chose to put on its front page an account of the Lewis Theater's victory over the Playboy's Sport Shop in the city black softball league championship.[72] The hometown support for the Eagles proved so small that the team moved the majority of its home games to Nashville, Tennessee, to finish out the 1950 season, while also cutting salaries.[73]

When the East-West game took place, three Eagles played for the West squad, outfielder Bob Harvey, pitcher Jehosie Heard, and infielder Curly Williams. Before the game, though, the NAL lost its best player, Elston Howard, to the New York Yankees. Representative of the overall decline in talent, Heard, the ace of Houston's pitching staff, made the All-Star game despite a record of six wins and eight losses.[74]

With the exception of the East-West game, by August college and high school football pushed the Eagles and African American baseball completely off the sports page. Without any fan support or newspaper coverage, the team limped through the remainder of its season, finishing the second half in last place with a record of five wins and seventeen losses.[75]

After the season ended, the *Houston Informer*'s sports page declared, "Negro Baseball on the Ropes."[76] The article claimed that black baseball faced a knockout without the help of the fans. Citing the Negro leagues as training grounds for African American players to learn the skills needed to play in the major leagues, the paper called for the sport's rescue. The danger sign was the low attendance at African American games. The American Giants, who played at Comiskey Park in Chicago, drew fewer than five thousand people per outing. Rumors circulated that the Baltimore Elite Giants, the 1949 champions, planned to cease operations. The Cleveland Buckeyes had already folded, and the Philadelphia Stars paid Satchel Paige one thousand dollars a game in an effort to attract fans, a gamble that lost money. The Negro American League also faced problems related to scheduling, the use of stadiums, and constantly increasing operating costs. If the teams failed to address these problems, the paper claimed, black baseball would not survive.[77]

To add insult to injury for the Eagles, four thousand fans turned out in Houston to watch Jackie Robinson's All-Stars play the Indianapolis Clowns in an exhibition game.[78] For the second year in a row, the Houston Eagles lost money. Despite team president Young's assertion that he liked Houston and wanted to stay, at the conclusion of the 1950 season the Eagles moved to New Orleans.

Management hoped New Orleans might prove the organization's salvation. Unfortunately, the team continued to lose money and disbanded permanently after the 1951 season.[79] The loss of the Houston Eagles marked the end of professional black baseball in Texas. The sport that for decades had served as a source of racial pride and identity for the Texas African American community now ceased to exist, taking with it the legacy of the Texas-Oklahoma-Louisiana League and such players as "Smokey" Joe Williams. The era of black professional baseball in Texas had come to a close.

The Lasting Legacy

8 The transfer of the Houston Eagles to New Orleans after the 1950 season marked the end of organized African American baseball in Texas. While a few black teams, such as the Abilene Black Eagles, continued to play at the local level throughout the next decade, the majority of Texas's semiprofessional African American teams ceased to exist. African Americans no longer looked to all-black teams as examples of their community or culture. With the end of segregated baseball in the country, the role black Texans played in shaping the Negro leagues came to an end. However, the impact of African Americans from the Lone Star State on the game of baseball continued.

Black Texans now directed their attention toward integrated professional baseball. In 1951, Cy Fausett, president of the Lamesa Lobos, whose team played in the Class C West Texas–New Mexico League, announced he planned to sign a black player, twenty-three-year-old shortstop J. W. Wingate. Wingate opened the season hitting safely in six straight games. However, he soon fell into a slump, stopped getting hits, and was cut by the team.[1]

Integration in the minor leagues brought challenges to the racial system throughout the country. Every time a team or league integrated, the spirit of Jackie Robinson was invoked.[2] For the Texas black community, the most important changes in baseball occurred at the minor league level.

The Texas League, the top minor league in the state, soon followed the example of the West Texas–New Mexico League, integrating in 1952. Dallas Eagles owner Dick Burnett, a prominent oilman, sought an African American player for his team. Burnett's motives for integrating the prominent southern league were more economic than humanitarian. He wanted to attract black fans, thus increasing team revenues, just as Jackie Robinson's presence had for the Brooklyn Dodgers. Burnett also wanted to find a player who would help the team win games. He eventually decided on pitcher Dave Hoskins.[3]

Hoskins began his baseball career as an outfielder in the Negro leagues but switched to pitching and even received instruction from Satchel Paige. He also proved a good player to break the color barrier in the Texas League because he understood the level of racism he would face. In 1944, Hoskins, along with Jackie Robinson and Sam Jethroe, received an invitation for a tryout with the Boston Red Sox and Boston Braves. Hoskins's team, the Homestead Grays, refused to let him attend. Even though he did not attend the tryout, the entire situation revealed to Hoskins the level of racism in Major League Baseball when both the Red Sox and the Braves stated that none of the men had sufficient talent.[4]

Hoskins also had experience as an integrator of an entire league. In 1948 he became the first African American to compete in the Central League, playing for a team in Grand Rapids, Michigan. The experience allowed him to handle the pressure of his first game in Texas on June 9, 1952, when he received three death threats that morning. The first letter claimed that Hoskins would be shot if he sat in the Dallas dugout. The second letter stated that Hoskins's murder was imminent if he walked onto the field. And the third death threat stated that any attempt by him to pitch in the game would result in his being shot.[5]

Hoskins played well for the Eagles, finishing the 1952 season with a record of twenty-two wins and ten losses, while batting .328.[6] He also provided a strong drawing card. The average fan attendance for Texas League games was two thousand to three thousand people in 1952, while games in which Hoskins played averaged six thousand spectators.[7] The number of black spectators at Eagles games when Hoskins pitched was so substantial that the African American section of Dallas's stadium could not accommodate them all. As a result, Burnett integrated the team's ballpark to maximize attendance and to keep from having to turn away any customer, regardless of skin color, who wanted to purchase a ticket.[8]

Hoskins provided black Texans with a visible example of their community and culture. Robinson and other African American major league players were still extremely popular, but black fans in Texas could actually watch Hoskins play on a regular basis. The fact that he excelled in games taking place in the largest cities in Texas made him a formidable counterargument to the state's system of segregation and racism that sought to denigrate African Americans.

With the Texas League's integration, a steady stream of black players from around the country played ball in Texas on their way to the majors, and served as further sources of racial pride and identity for the state's black community. But though the teams were now integrated, the black players in the Texas League still faced problems in the segregated South during the 1950s and 1960s. Manny Mota, a Dominican Republic native who played in the Texas League in 1962, recalled that at one restaurant the owner brandished a shotgun to emphasize his refusal to serve Mota.[9] Cito Gaston, who played for Austin and went on to manage the Toronto Blue Jays to World Series championships in 1992 and 1993, remembered that when the Austin team ate at the bus station in Amarillo, he and the other black players were forced to eat behind the restaurant.[10] While these African American players faced racial problems up through the 1960s, they still left their impact on society and the game of baseball. They brought integration to much of Texas, including the hotels and restaurants used by the Texas League teams. Furthermore, players like Gaston carried their Texas League experiences with them to the major leagues, where they helped shape baseball.

African American players challenged segregation throughout the country, and especially in the South. With thirteen of the eighteen teams training in the state of Florida, most teams refused to challenge the existing system of racial segregation. As a result, African Americans on the teams stayed in the homes of local citizens, or boarding houses in African American neighborhoods. However, beginning in 1961, these players and their teams demanded that black players be allowed to stay in hotels and be included in events such as the St. Petersburg "Salute to Baseball" breakfast that hosted the St. Louis Cardinals every year.[11] Walter White, the executive director of the NAACP, stated that the "most visible sign of change to most Americans is the cracking of the color line in professional baseball."[12]

With integration, African American players from Texas began to join major league teams. Ernie Banks, the former star shortstop for the Dallas Black Giants, became the first African American to play for the Chicago

Cubs. Banks, who played briefly with the Kansas City Monarchs before entering the military, redefined the position of shortstop with his hitting ability and power at the plate. During a major league career that lasted from 1953 until 1971, Banks hit 512 home runs, posted a career batting average of .274, played in eleven All-Star games, and won a Gold Glove award in 1960. He also became the first player to win back-to-back Most Valuable Player awards, receiving the National League honor in 1958 and 1959. Banks became synonymous with the Chicago Cubs, eventually being enshrined in the National Baseball Hall of Fame in 1976.[13]

Banks continued the role begun by earlier players, such as Willie Wells, of defining the African American community in Texas. And in baseball, he changed the image of shortstop, conventionally viewed as of little offensive importance, by his powerful, dominant presence at the plate. The model set by Banks became the standard for the position during the late 1990s and early 2000s.

Other Texans followed the model set by Banks, defining the Texas black community and influencing baseball through their success in the major leagues, some earning election to the Hall of Fame. Frank Robinson, from Beaumont, became the first person to receive the Most Valuable Player award in both the National and American Leagues. He first won the award with the Cincinnati Reds in 1961 and then again with the Baltimore Orioles in 1966. Robinson also became the first African American manager of a major league team, leading the Cleveland Indians from 1975 to 1977.[14] Robinson managed and worked in front-office jobs in major league baseball for the remainder of his career. His accomplishments in administrative positions exemplified African American intelligence and refuted racist theories that argued African Americans were not smart enough to hold such positions not just in baseball but in all segments of American business.

Another influential black Texan and Hall of Fame player, Joe Morgan of Bonham, began his professional baseball career with San Antonio of the Texas League. Morgan went on to play for the Houston Colt .45s, Texas's first major league team, as well as the Cincinnati Reds, San Francisco Giants, Philadelphia Phillies, and Oakland Athletics. He led the Cincinnati Reds to victories in the World Series in 1975 and 1976, also earning the National League Most Valuable Player award both years.[15]

Morgan and Robinson were the only two of the eleven African Americans from Texas in the National Baseball Hall of Fame not to play in the

Negro leagues. These eleven black players largely account for the high number of Texans in the Hall of Fame. Only four white players from Texas have been elected.

Still another African American from Texas to achieve great success at the professional level was Austin native Don Baylor, who won the Most Valuable Player award for the American League in 1978 with the California Angels. He later became the first manager of the Colorado Rockies, taking the team to its first playoff appearance.[16]

With the arrival in 1961 of the National League's Houston Colt .45s, later the Houston Astros, and the Texas Rangers of the American League in 1972, black Texans continued to shape baseball. Fans now followed the accomplishments of blacks on Texas's professional teams, players such as J. R. Richard of the Astros and Ferguson Jenkins and Al Oliver of the Rangers. These professional teams and players established new heroes and models for black Texans. But new generations of African American fans forgot about players such as "Smokey" Joe Williams and Willie Wells, who previously filled these roles.

As the public's knowledge of black baseball in Texas faded, an important part of African American history disappeared. For more than fifty years, black semiprofessional teams provided entertainment for countless African Americans. Teams such as the Lubbock Black Hubbers and the Abilene Black Eagles stimulated community pride and identity.

Rube Foster brought recognition to Texas and influenced the game of baseball as a pitcher, manager, and founder of the Negro National League. Texas's reputation grew as players such as "Smokey" Joe Williams dominated black baseball. The state became known as one of the premier homes for African American baseball in the country. Black Texans in general felt their community uplifted, and black men in particular felt their masculinity reaffirmed in the face of the racial segregation in the state.

By the 1960s and 1970s, excitement over the Texas Rangers and the Houston Astros replaced that felt for the Texas-Oklahoma-Louisiana League forty years before. As fans in Texas watched the Rangers struggle through the 1970s as one of the worst teams in baseball, the memory of the Houston Black Buffaloes, champions of the Texas-Oklahoma-Louisiana League in 1929 and 1930, remained lost in the annals of history. The players who survived from the old African American teams in Texas worked in obscurity outside of the sport. Pat Patterson, former outfielder for the Houston

Eagles, served as a high school teacher, coach, athletics director, and super-intendent in Houston.[17] Frazier Robinson, who started with the Abilene Black Eagles in 1936, worked as a janitor in Los Angeles after he retired from the Negro leagues in 1953.[18]

In the new world of integrated baseball, few people mourned the loss of segregated teams. However, also lost was a vibrant culture that domi-nated and defined African American life for more than fifty years. Within this microcosm of African American life, different groups sought different goals through the sport of baseball. The middle-class team owners sought to make a profit, while the working-class players performed for the enjoy-ment of the game, as well as the opportunity to achieve a level of public acclaim and admiration normally beyond their reach. For the professional player, the salaries offered in black baseball exceeded the average salaries for most jobs available to African Americans at the time.

While the memory of segregated baseball has faded, its importance is still evident. What made black baseball in Texas significant was the fact that it occurred entirely within the African American community. Within this sphere the efforts of the middle-class team owners and working-class players provided a valuable source of entertainment, racial pride, cultural expression, and a positive image of black masculinity for that community. But more than that, African American baseball in Texas gave black Texans the opportunity to influence the game of baseball, the cultural history of Texas, and the culture and history of the whole country.

Appendix

NEGRO LEAGUE VETERANS WHO PLAYED IN TEXAS[1]

PLAYER	TEXAS TEAM/CONNECTION	DATES
Albright, Thomas "Pistol Pete"	Born in Crockett, Texas	1909
Allen, Newton "Newt"	Born in Austin, Texas	1901
Bailey, Otha "Bill"	Houston Eagles	1950
* Banks, Ernie	Dallas Black Giants	1949
Barbee, Quincy	Pampa Oilers of the integrated West Texas–New Mexico League	1952
Bassett, Lloyd "Pepper"	Austin Black Senators	1935
Bell, William	Born in Galveston	1897
Bennett, Sam	Austin Black Senators	1910
Beverly, William (Bill) "Fireball"	Houston Eagles	1950
Blackmon, Henry	Texas All-Stars San Antonio Black Aces	1917 1920
Brooks, Henry	Houston Eagles	1949–1950
Brown, David "Lefty"	Dallas Black Giants	1917–1918
Brown, James (Jim)	San Marcos Giants	1918
Brown, Jerome	Houston Eagles	1949

* Inducted into National Baseball Hall of Fame

PLAYER	TEXAS TEAM/CONNECTION	DATES
Carter, Marlin	San Antonio Black Indians	1931
* Cooper, Andy	Born in Waco, Texas	1896
Cooper, Daltie	Born in Waco, Texas	around 1900
Cunningham, Larry	Houston Eagles	1950
Danbridge, John	Houston Eagles	1949
Davis, John Howard (Johnny) "Cherokee"	Houston Eagles	1949–1950
Davis, Saul Henry (Sol) "Rareback"	Houston Black Buffaloes	1918–1922
Douglas, Jesse Warren	Born in Longview, Texas	1920
Douglass, Edward (Eddie)	Dallas	1907
* Foster, Andrew "Rube"	Waco Yellow Jackets	1900
* Foster, William (Bill, Willie)	Born in Calvert, Texas	1904
Gatewood, William "Big Bill"	Born in San Antonio	1881
Gibson, Welda	Houston Eagles	1949–1950
Gipson, Alvin "Bubba," "Skeet"	Houston Eagles	1949
Golden, Clyde	Houston Eagles	1949–1950
Grace, William (Willie)	Houston Eagles	1950
Grigs, Wiley	Houston Eagles	1950
Handy, George	Houston Eagles	1949
Harvey, Robert A. (Bob)	Houston Eagles	1949–1950
Haynes, Willie	Dallas Black Giants	1921
Heard, Jehosie "Jay"	Houston Eagles	1949–1950
Hill, Johnson (John) "Fred"	Played semipro in Texas	1910s
Holloway, Christopher Columbus "Crush"	Born in Hillsboro	1896
Hooker, Lenial Charlie (Lennie, Len)	Houston Eagles	1949
Hubbard, Jess James "Mountain"	Houston Black Oilers	1915
Hudsperth, Robert (Bob) "Highpockets"	San Antonio Black Aces	1920
Jackman, Will (Bill) "Earl"	Played semipro in Texas	1910s
Johnson, George Washington "Dibo"	Fort Worth Wonders	1909

* Inducted into National Baseball Hall of Fame

PLAYER	TEXAS TEAM/CONNECTION	DATES
Jones, Lee	Dallas Giants	1908
Jones, Reuben	Dallas Giants	1918
Jones, Reuben	Houston Eagles	1948
Lacy, Raymond	Houston Eagles	1949–1950
Lewis, Rufus	Houston Eagles	1949–1950
* Mackey, Raleigh "Biz"	San Antonio Black Aces	1918
Mason, Ed	Wichita Falls Black Spudders	1929–1930
McClure, Robert (Bob) "Big Boy"	San Antonio Black Aces	1920
McNeal, Clyde	Lonnie Greene's All-Stars	1944
Parnell, Roy "Red"	Houston Black Buffaloes	1932
Patterson, Bob	San Antonio Black Indians	1929
Patterson, William	Houston Black Buffaloes Austin Senators	1917–1925
Robinson, Frazier "Slow"	Abilene Black Eagles	1936
Ruffin, Charles "Leon"	Houston Eagles	1949–1950
* Santop, Louis "Top," "Big Bertha"	Fort Worth Wonders	1909
Smith, Henry	In Texas Negro League	1930s
* Smith, Hilton	Austin Senators	1931
Walker, George T.	San Antonio Shepherds	1930s
Washington, Namon	San Antonio Black Aces	1920
* Wells, Willie "El Diablo"	San Antonio Black Aces	1923
Wickware, Frank	Dallas Black Giants	1909
Wilkes, James (Jimmy)	Houston Eagles	1949–1950
Williams, Chester	Houston Black Buffaloes	1929
Williams, Jesse	Mineola Black Spiders	Late 1920s to early 1930s
* Williams, Joseph (Joe) "Smokey Joe"	San Antonio Black Broncos	1907–1909
Williams, Morris	San Antonio Black Broncos	1920
Wright, Zollie	Dallas Black Giants	1930

* *Inducted into National Baseball Hall of Fame*

Notes

CHAPTER 1

1. Frederick Douglass, *My Bondage and My Freedom* (New York: Dover, 1969), 252.

2. David Wiggins, "Good Times on the Old Plantation: Popular Recreations of the Black Slave in Antebellum South, 1810–1860," *Journal of Sports History* 4, no. 3 (Fall 1977): 266.

3. Ibid., 268.

4. David Wiggins, "The Play of Slave Children in the Plantation Communities of the Old South," *Journal of Sports History* 7, no. 2 (Summer 1980): 21–22.

5. Geoffrey C. Ward and Ken Burns, *Baseball: An Illustrated History* (New York: Knopf, 1994), 4.

6. Ibid., 5.

7. Mark Ribowsky, *A Complete History of the Negro Leagues: 1884 to 1955* (Secaucus, NJ: Carol Publishing Group, 1995), 13.

8. Lawrence D. Hogan, *Shades of Glory: The Negro Leagues and the Story of African American Baseball* (Washington DC: National Geographic, 2006), 14, 17; Michael E. Lomax, *Black Baseball Entrepreneurs, 1860–1901: Operating by Any Means Necessary* (Syracuse, NY: Syracuse University Press, 2003), 14.

9. John Carroll, "Abner Doubleday Strikes Out Again: The Origins of Baseball in Southeast Texas," *North American Society for Sports History: Proceedings and Newsletter*, 1986, 45.

10. Mary Lou LeCompte, "Any Sunday in April: The Rise of Sports in San Antonio and the Hispanic Borderlands," *Journal of Sports History* 13, no. 2 (Summer 1986): 143–144.

11. Ward and Burns, *Baseball*, 20.

12. Ibid., 23–24, 26.

13. LeCompte, "Any Sunday in April," 145.

14. Leslie A. Heaphy, *The Negro Leagues:1869–1960* (Jefferson, NC: McFarland and Co., 2003).

15. Gwendolyn Captain, "Enter Ladies and Gentlemen of Color: Gender, Sport, and the Ideal of African American Manhood and Womanhood during the Late Nineteenth and Early Twentieth Centuries," *Journal of Sports History* 18, no. 1 (Spring 1991): 81–84.

16. Elliot Gorn, "Gender, Class, and Sports in Late Nineteenth Century America," *North American Society for Sports History: Proceedings and Newsletter*, 1990, 42.

17. Hogan, *Shades of Glory*, 21–22.

18. "Play Ball! Texas Baseball," Bob Bullock Texas State Historical Museum, 14 June 2003–4 January 2004.

19. Captain, "Enter Ladies and Gentlemen of Color," 91.

20. John Holway, *Blackball Stars: Negro League Pioneers* (New York: Carroll and Graf, 1988), 61.

21. George Forkerway, interview by author, 19 August 1999.

CHAPTER 2

1. Rob Ruck, *Sandlot Seasons: Sport in Black Pittsburgh* (Urbana: University of Illinois Press, 1993), 3.

2. Ibid., 39.

3. Ibid., 40.

4. Ibid., 41.

5. Ruben "Jellie" Samuel, interview by Patsy Colvert, 5 February 2001, tape recording, T.L.L. Temple Memorial Library, Lufkin, Texas.

6. Forkerway, interview by author.

7. Samuel, interview by Colvert.

8. Ibid.

9. John Holway, *Voices from the Great Black Baseball Leagues* (New York: De Capo Press, 1975), 63.

10. Ruck, *Sandlot Seasons*, 45.

11. *Dallas Express*, 7 June 1919.

12. Samuel, interview by Colvert.

13. *Dallas Express*, 30 August 1919.

14. Ibid., 17 May 1919.

15. Forkerway, interview by author.

16. Holway, *Voices from the Great Black Baseball Leagues*, 64.

17. *Dallas Express*, 24 May 1919.

18. Ibid., 23 August 1919.

19. Samuel, interview by Colvert.

20. Michael Lomax, "Black Entrepreneurship in the National Pastime: The Rise of Semiprofessional Baseball in Black Chicago, 1890–1915," *Journal of Sports History* 25, no. 1 (Spring 1998): 43–44.

21. Ibid., 45.

22. Gerald Gems, "Great Wasn't Good Enough: The Black Sports Experience in Chicago," *North American Society for Sports History: Proceedings and Newsletter*, 1991, 48.

23. Steven Riess, "The Baseball Magnates and Urban Politics in the Progressive Era: 1895–1920," *Journal of Sports History* 1, no. 1 (1974): 41.

24. Lomax, "Black Entrepreneurship," 43.

25. *Dallas Express*, 27 March 1920.

26. Ibid., 13 April 1920.

27. Ibid., 17 April 1920.

28. Ibid., 10 April 1920.

29. Ibid., 24 April 1920.

30. Alwyn Barr, *Black Texans: A History of African Americans in Texas, 1528–1995* (Norman: University of Oklahoma Press, 1996), 134.

31. Rob Fink, "Black College Football in Texas," PhD diss., Texas Tech University, 2003, 63–64.

32. *Houston Informer*, 5 March 1921.

33. Ibid.

34. Ibid., 26 March 1921.

35. *Dallas Express*, 12 March 1921.

36. Ibid., 9 April 1921.

37. Ibid., 23 April 1921.

38. *Houston Informer*, 14 May 1921.

39. Ibid.

40. Ibid., 21 May 1921.

41. *Dallas Express*, 27 May 1922.

42. Ibid.

43. Holway, *Voices from the Great Black Baseball Leagues*, 64.

44. *Houston Informer*, 28 May 1921.

45. Samuel, interview by Colvert.

46. *Houston Informer*, 4 June 1921.

47. Ibid.

48. *Dallas Express*, 9 September 1922.

49. *Houston Informer,* 7 April 1923.
50. Ibid., 21 April 1923.
51. *Dallas Express,* 5 May 1923.
52. *Houston Informer,* 31 March 1923.
53. *Dallas Express,* 14 July 1923.
54. Ibid., 18 August 1923.
55. Ibid.
56. *Houston Informer,* 26 May 1923.
57. Ibid.
58. Ibid.
59. Ibid., 30 June 1923.
60. Ibid.
61. Ibid., 5 April 1924.
62. Ibid., 26 April 1924.
63. Ibid., 22 August 1925.

CHAPTER 3

1. James A. Riley, *The Biographical Encyclopedia of the Negro Baseball Leagues* (New York: Carroll and Graf, 1994), s.v. "Foster, Andrew."

2. Robert Peterson, *Only the Ball Was White: A History of Legendary Black Players and All-Black Professional Teams* (New York: Oxford University Press, 1970), 104.

3. Robert Cottrell, *Black Ball, the Black Sox, and the Babe: Baseball's Crucial 1920 Season* (Jefferson, NC: McFarland and Co., 2002), 61.

4. Ribowsky, *Complete History,* 54.

5. Lomax, "Black Entrepreneurship in the National Pastime," 48.

6. Robert Cottrell, *The Best Pitcher in Baseball: The Life of Rube Foster, Negro League Giant* (New York: New York University Press, 2001), 10.

7. Cottrell, *Best Pitcher in Baseball,* 10; Riley, *Biographical Encyclopedia,* s.v. "Foster, Andrew."

8. *Indianapolis Freeman,* 13 November 1909.

9. Riley, *Biographical Encyclopedia,* s.v. "Foster, Andrew."

10. Andrew Foster, "How to Pitch," *Sol White's History of Colored Base Ball, with Other Documents on the Early Black Game: 1886–1936,* ed. Jerry Malloy (Lincoln: University of Nebraska Press, 1995), 96.

11. Ibid.
12. Ibid., 99.
13. Ibid.
14. Ibid., 100.
15. Ibid.
16. Cottrell, *Blackball, the Black Sox, and the Babe,* 61.

17. *Houston Informer*, 16 March 1929.

18. Donn Rogosin, *Invisible Men: Life in Baseball's Negro Leagues* (New York: Kodansha International, 1983), 8.

19. Ribowsky, *Complete History*, 67.

20. Holway, *Blackball Stars*, 8–9.

21. *Pittsburgh Courier*, 16 January 1926.

22. Ribowsky, *Complete History*, 70.

23. Ibid.

24. *Indianapolis Freeman*, 17 July 1909.

25. Ibid., 7 August 1909.

26. Ribowsky, *Complete History*, 70.

27. *Indianapolis Freeman*, 18 October 1909.

28. Hogan, *Shades of Glory*, 112.

29. Paul Debono, *The Chicago American Giants* (Jefferson, NC: McFarland and Co., 2007), 33.

30. *Indianapolis Freeman*, 20 November 1909.

31. Larry Lester, "Andrew 'Rube' Foster: Gem of a Man," *Black Baseball in Chicago: Essays on the Players, Teams and Games of the Negro Leagues Most Important City*, ed. Leslie A. Heaphy (Jefferson, NC: McFarland and Co., 2006), 151.

32. Peterson, *Only the Ball Was White*, 108.

33. *Chicago Defender*, 2 April 1910.

34. Ibid., 16 April 1910.

35. Cottrell, *Best Pitcher in Baseball*, 46.

36. Ibid.

37. Ribowsky, *Complete History*, 72.

38. Ibid., 80.

39. Ibid., 85.

40. Ibid., 75.

41. Hogan, *Shades of Glory*, 113–114.

42. Ibid., 132–133.

43. *Indianapolis Freeman*, 7 August 1915.

44. Ibid., 14 August 1915.

45. Ibid.

46. Ribowsky, *Complete History*, 91.

47. *Indianapolis Freeman*, 24 July 1915.

48. Ibid., 7 August 1915.

49. Ibid.

50. Ibid.

51. Ibid.

52. Ibid.

53. Ibid., 14 August 1915.

54. Ibid.

55. Ibid., 12 May 1917.

56. Ibid., 19 May 1917.

57. Ribowsky, *Complete History*, 93.

58. *Indianapolis Freeman*, 4 August 1917.

59. Holway, *Voices from the Great Black Baseball Leagues*, 47.

60. *Indianapolis Freeman*, 12 January 1918.

61. Ribowsky, *Complete History*, 107.

62. Cottrell, *Best Pitcher in Baseball*, 144–145.

63. Cottrell, *Blackball, the Black Sox, and the Babe*, 147–148.

64. *Indianapolis Freeman*, 21 February 1920.

65. Ibid., 20 March 1920.

66. Peterson, *Only the Ball Was White*, 89.

67. Ibid., 87.

68. Ribowsky, *Complete History*, 108.

69. William Brashler, *The Story of Negro League Baseball* (New York: Ticknor and Fields, 1994), 36.

70. *Pittsburgh Courier*, 30 January 1926.

71. Ribowsky, *Complete History*, 108.

72. Ibid., 109.

73. Ibid., 122–123.

74. *Houston Informer*, 18 September 1926.

75. Holway, *Blackball Stars*, 33.

76. Ibid.

77. *Pittsburgh Courier*, 9 September 1926.

CHAPTER 4

1. William McNeil, *Cool Papas and Double Duties: The All-Time Greats of the Negro Leagues* (Jefferson, NC: McFarland and Co., 2001), 109–110.

2. Riley, *Biographical Encyclopedia*, s.v. "Santop, Louis."

3. Larry Lester, *Baseball's First Colored World Series: The 1924 Meeting of the Hilldale Giants and Kansas City Monarchs* (Jefferson, NC: McFarland and Co., 2006), 37.

4. "Just Deserts," *Texas Highways*, December 2001, 45.

5. McNeil, *Cool Papas and Double Duties*, 112–113.

6. Riley, *Biographical Encyclopedia*, s.v. "Cooper, Andy."

7. Janet Bruce, *The Kansas City Monarchs: Champions of Black Baseball* (Lawrence: University Press of Kansas, 1985), 55.

8. *Pittsburgh Courier*, 12 April 1952.

9. Holway, *Blackball Stars*, 61.

10. Ibid.

11. Ibid.

12. Peterson, *Only the Ball Was White*, 5.

13. Ibid.

14. Holway, *Blackball Stars*, 63.

15. Ibid.

16. Ibid.

17. Riley, *Biographical Encyclopedia*, s.v. "Williams, Joseph."

18. *Indianapolis Freeman*, 12 June 1909.

19. Hogan, *Shades of Glory*, 121.

20. Riley, *Biographical Encyclopedia*, s.v. "Williams, Joseph."

21. *Indianapolis Freeman*, 10 September 1910.

22. Ibid., 17 September 1910.

23. Peterson, *Only the Ball Was White*, 70.

24. Holway, *Blackball Stars*, 65.

25. Ibid., 66.

26. Ibid., 67.

27. Ibid., 68.

28. Buck O'Neil, *I Was Right on Time: My Journey from the Negro Leagues to the Majors* (New York: Simon and Schuster, 1996), 139.

29. Brashler, *Story of Negro League Baseball*, 31.

30. *Chicago Defender*, 11 April 1914.

31. Holway, *Blackball Stars*, 69.

32. Ibid., 71.

33. Ibid., 70–71.

34. Ibid., 69.

35. Ibid.

36. Rogosin, *Invisible Men*, 78.

37. Brad Snyder, *Beyond the Shadow of the Senators: The Untold Story of the Homestead Grays and the Integration of Baseball* (Chicago: Contemporary Books, 2003), 37–38.

38. *Pittsburgh Courier*, 13 February 1926.

39. Ibid., 9 October 1926.

40. Holway, *Blackball Stars*, 73.

41. O'Neil, *I Was Right on Time*, 140.

42. John Holway, *Black Diamonds: Life in the Negro Leagues from the Men Who Lived It* (New York: Stadium Books, 1991), 28.

43. Peterson, *Only the Ball Was White*, 163.

44. Snyder, *Beyond the Shadow of the Senators*, 28

45. Ibid., 44.

46. Holway, *Blackball Stars*, 76.

47. *Austin American-Statesman*, 2 March 1999.

48. Peterson, *Only the Ball Was White*, 223.

49. Riley, *Biographical Encyclopedia*, s.v. "Mackey, Raleigh."

50. Ribowsky, *Complete History*, 116.

51. Holway, *Blackball Stars*, 221.

52. Riley, *Biographical Encyclopedia*, s.v. "Mackey, Raleigh."

53. Ibid.

54. Ibid., 504.

55. Hogan, *Shades of Glory*, 158.

56. Lester, *Baseball's First Colored World Series*, 74.

57. Holway, *Blackball Stars*, 222.

58. Ibid., 221.

59. Ibid., 223.

60. Ibid.

61. Riley, *Biographical Encyclopedia*, s.v. "Mackey, Raleigh."

62. Holway, *Blackball Stars*, 226.

63. Ibid., 227.

64. Riley, *Biographical Encyclopedia*, s.v. "Mackey, Raleigh."

65. Holway, *Blackball Stars*, 230.

66. Ibid.

67. Riley, *Biographical Encyclopedia*, s.v. "Mackey, Raleigh."

68. Ibid.

69. Lester, *Baseball's First Colored World Series*, 74.

70. Peterson, *Only the Ball Was White*, 234.

71. Art Rust, Jr., *Get That Nigger Off the Field: The Oral History of the Negro Leagues* (Brooklyn: Book Mail Services, 1976), 26.

72. Peterson, *Only the Ball Was White*, 234.

73. Holway, *Blackball Stars*, 219.

74. Rogosin, *Invisible Men*, 40.

75. Ibid., 41.

76. Ibid.

77. Ibid.

78. Ibid.

79. Ibid.

80. Ibid., 42.

81. Riley, *Biographical Encyclopedia*, s.v. "Wells, Willie."

82. Holway, *Black Diamonds*, 123.

83. Riley, *Biographical Encyclopedia*, s.v. "Wells, Willie."

84. Ibid.

85. Ibid.

86. Rogosin, *Invisible Men*, 25.

87. Ribowsky, *Complete History*, 168.

88. Rogosin, *Invisible Men*, 25.

89. Holway, *Blackball Stars*, 359.

90. Rogosin, *Invisible Men*, 72.

91. Ibid., 73.

92. Ibid., 59–60.

93. Ibid., 171.

94. Riley, *Biographical Encyclopedia*, s.v. "Wells, Willie."

95. Brashler, *Story of Negro League Baseball*, 69.

96. Riley, *Biographical Encyclopedia*, s.v. "Wells, Willie."

97. Bob Luke, *Willie Wells: "El Diablo of the Negro Leagues* (Austin: University of Texas Press, 2007), 25; Rogosin, *Invisible Men*, 74.

98. Riley, *Biographical Encyclopedia*, s.v. "Wells, Willie."

99. *Houston Informer*, 7 May 1949.

100. O'Neil, *I Was Right on Time*, 144.

101. Riley, *Biographical Encyclopedia*, s.v. "Wells, Willie."

102. *Austin American-Statesman*, 19 January 1998.

103. Luke, *Willie Wells*, 5, 143–146.

CHAPTER 5

1. *Houston Informer*, 19 January 1929.

2. Ibid., 2 February 1929.

3. Ibid.

4. Ibid.

5. Howard Beeth and Cary D. Wintz, *Black Dixie: Afro-Texan History and Culture in Houston* (College Station: Texas A&M University Press, 1992), 109.

6. Peggy Hardman, "Strickland, Henry," *New Handbook of Texas* (Austin: Texas State Historical Association, 1996), 124.

7. Darwin Payne, *Big D: Triumph and Troubles of an American Super City in the Twentieth Century* (Dallas: Tree Forks Press, 1994), 180.

8. *Houston Informer*, 2 February 1929.

9. Ibid.

10. Ibid., 23 February 1929.

11. Ibid.

12. Ibid.

13. Ibid.

14. Ibid., 9 March 1929.

15. U.S. Department of Commerce, *Negroes in the United States: 1920–1932*, by Charles E. Hall (Washington, DC: Government Printing Office, 1935), 141.

16. *Houston Informer*, 9 March 1929.

17. Ibid., 16 March 1929.

18. Ibid.

19. Ibid., 6 April 1929.

20. Ibid., 20 April 1929.

21. Ibid., 27 April 1929.

22. Ibid.

23. Ibid.

24. Bruce A. Glasrud, "William M. McDonald," *Black Leaders: Texans for their Times*, ed. Alwyn Barr and Robert A. Calvert (Austin: Texas State Historical Association, 1981), 91.

25. *Houston Informer*, 4 May 1929.

26. Ibid.

27. Ibid.

28. Ibid.

29. Ibid., 18 May 1929.

30. Ibid.

31. Ibid., 25 May 1929.

32. Ibid., 1 June 1929.

33. Ibid.

34. Ibid.

35. Ibid., 22 June 1929.

36. Ibid.

37. Ibid.

38. Ibid., 13 July 1929.

39. Ibid.

40. Ibid., 20 July 1929.

41. Ibid., 14 September 1929.

42. Alan Govenar, *Portraits of Community: African American Photography in Texas* (Austin: Texas State Historical Association, 1996), 18–19.

43. *Houston Informer*, 21 September 1929.

44. Ibid.

45. Ibid., 28 September 1929.

46. Ibid., 5 October 1929.

47. Ibid., 29 March 1930.

48. Ribowsky, *Complete History*, 142.

49. Holway, *Voices from the Great Black Baseball Leagues*, 195.

50. Barr, *Black Texans*, 153–154.

51. *Houston Informer*, 30 March 1930.

52. Ibid., 5 April 1930.

53. Ibid., 26 April 1930.

54. Ibid., 3 May, 1930.

55. Ibid., 10 May 1930.

56. Ibid., 2 August 1930.

57. Ibid.

58. Ribowsky, *Complete History*, 144–145.

59. *Houston Informer*, 4 October 1930.

60. Ibid.

61. Ibid., 21 February 1931.

62. Diana J. Klainen, "White, Julius," *New Handbook of Texas* (Austin: Texas State Historical Association), 929.

63. *Houston Informer*, 11 April 1931.

64. Hogan, *Shades of Glory*, 238.

65. *San Antonio Register*, 29 May 1931.

66. Ibid.

CHAPTER 6

1. *Houston Informer*, 13 February 1932.

2. *San Antonio Register*, 1 April 1932.

3. Ibid., 24 June 1932.

4. Ruck, *Sandlot Seasons*, 78.

5. *San Antonio Register*, 5 August 1932.

6. Ibid., 2 September 1932.

7. Ribowsky, *Complete History*, 142.

8. Holway, *Voices from the Great Black Baseball Leagues*, 99–101.

9. Barr, *Black Texans*, 153–155.

10. *Houston Informer*, 23 February 1935.

11. U.S. Bureau of the Census, *Statistical Abstract of the U.S.: 1950* (Washington, DC: Government Printing Office, 1950), 75–78.

12. *Houston Informer*, 23 March 1935.

13. Ibid., 6 April 1935.

14. Barr, *Black Texans*, 153.

15. *Houston Informer*, 25 May 1935.

16. Ibid.

17. Ibid.

18. Ibid.

19. Ibid., 17 May 1935.

20. Ibid.

21. Carlton Priestly and George Woods, interview by Robert Foster, 9 April 1969, interview 1A, tape recording, Southwest Collection, Texas Tech University, Lubbock.

22. Ibid.

23. Barr, *Black Texans*, 155.

24. *Houston Informer*, 1 June 1935.

25. Ibid.

26. Ibid., 8 June 1935.

27. Ibid., 22 June 1935.

28. Ibid.

29. Ibid.

30. Ibid., 6 July 1935.

31. Ibid., 13 July 1935.

32. Ribowsky, *Complete History*, 207.

33. *Houston Informer*, 22 February 1936.

34. Ibid., 28 March 1936.

35. Ibid., 2 May 1936.

36. Ibid., 30 May 1936.

37. Ibid., 13 June 1936.

38. Ibid., 20 June 1936.

39. *San Antonio Register*, 2 July 1937.

40. George Eubank, interview by Robert Foster, 16 April 1969, interview 1A, tape recording, Southwest Collection, Texas Tech University, Lubbock.

41. *San Antonio Register*, 24 September 1937.

42. Holway, *Voices from the Great Black Leagues*, 235.

43. Ribowsky, *Complete History*, 209.

44. *San Antonio Register*, 15 May 1936.

45. Samuel Regalado, "Incarcerated Sport: Nisei Women's Softball and Athletics during Japanese American Interment," *Journal of Sports History* 27, no. 3 (Fall 2000): 431.

46. *San Antonio Register*, 31 July 1941.

47. Holway, *Voices from the Great Black Baseball Leagues*, 259.

48. *Houston Informer*, 10 March 1945.

49. Ibid., 7 July 1945.

50. Ibid., 28 July 1945.

51. Ibid., 8 September 1945.

52. Ibid., 1 September 1945.

53. Ibid., 6 October 1945.

54. Ibid., 5 March 1946.

55. Ibid., 23 March 1946.

56. *San Antonio Register*, 3 May 1946.

57. Hogan, *Shades of Glory*, 346.

58. *Houston Informer*, 22 March 1947.

59. Ibid., 31 May 1947.

60. Ibid., 13 April 1948.

61. Ibid., 20 April 1948.

62. Ibid., 12 June 1948.

63. Ibid.

64. *Dallas Express,* 13 March 1948.

65. *Houston Informer,* 1 January 1949.

66. Ibid., 29 January 1949.

67. *Dallas Express,* 14 May 1949.

68. *Houston Informer,* 21 May 1949.

69. Samuel, interview by Colvert.

70. *Dallas Express,* 28 May 1949.

71. Ibid., 11 June 1949.

72. Ibid., 25 June 1949.

73. Ibid., 22 July 1949.

74. Bill O'Neal, *The Texas League: 1888–1987, A Century of Baseball* (Austin: Eakin Press, 1987), 108–109.

75. Samuel, interview by Colvert.

76. Damon Hill, interview by David Murrah, 26 June 1975, interview 1A, tape recording, Southwest Collection, Texas Tech University, Lubbock.

77. Forkerway, interview by author.

78. Samuel Regalado, "Baseball in the Barrio," *North American Society for Sports History: Proceedings and Newsletter,* 1985, 28.

CHAPTER 7

1. Steve Bullock, "Playing for Their Nation: The American Military and Baseball during World War II," *Journal of Sports History* 27, no. 1 (Spring 2000): 67–68.

2. Daniel Nathan, "Sugar Ray Robinson, the Sweet Science, and the Politics of Meaning," *Journal of Sports History* 26, no. 1 (Spring 1999): 164.

3. Bullock, "Playing for Their Nation," 74.

4. *Houston Informer,* 6 October 1945.

5. Barr, *Black Texans,* 174–175.

6. *Houston Informer,* 22 March 1947.

7. Ibid.

8. William Simmons, "Jackie Robinson and the American Mind: Journalistic Perceptions of the Reintegration of Baseball," *Journal of Sports History* 12, no. 1 (Spring 1985): 40.

9. David Wiggins, "Wendell Smith, the *Pittsburgh Courier-Journal,* and the Campaign to Include Blacks in Organized Baseball, 1933–1945," *Journal of Sports History* 10, no. 2 (Summer 1983): 5.

10. Henry D. Fetter, "The Party Line and the Color Line: The American Communist Party, the *Daily Worker,* and Jackie Robinson," *Journal of Sports History* 25, no. 3 (Fall 1998): 375.

11. Ribowsky, *Complete History*, 297.

12. *Houston Informer*, 20 April 1948.

13. Ribowsky, *Complete History*, 285.

14. Larry Gerlach, "Baseball's Other Great Experiment: Eddie Klep and the Integration of the Negro Leagues," *Journal of Sports History* 25, no. 3 (Fall 1998): 453, 456, 459, 467.

15. Ribowsky, *Complete History*, 285.

16. Ibid., 306.

17. Ibid.

18. U.S. Bureau of the Census, *Statistical Abstract of the U.S.: 1950* (Washington, DC: Government Printing Office, 1960), 55.

19. *Houston Informer*, 26 March 1949.

20. *Dallas Express*, 25 March 1949.

21. *Houston Informer*, 30 April 1949.

22. Ibid., 7 May 1949.

23. Ibid.

24. Ibid.

25. Ibid.

26. Barr, *Black Texans*, 185.

27. Ibid., 215.

28. *Houston Informer*, 14 May 1949.

29. Ibid.

30. Ibid., 21 May 1949.

31. Ibid., 28 May 1949.

32. Ibid., 11 June 1949.

33. Ibid.

34. *Dallas Express*, 28 May 1949.

35. *Houston Informer*, 11 June 1949.

36. Ibid., 25 June 1949.

37. Ibid.

38. Ibid., 2 July 1949.

39. *Dallas Express*, 11 June 1949.

40. *Houston Informer*, 2 July 1949.

41. Ibid., 9 July 1949.

42. *Dallas Express*, 22 July 1949.

43. *Houston Informer*, 20 August 1949.

44. *San Antonio Register*, 8 July 1949.

45. *Houston Informer*, 3 September 1949.

46. *Dallas Express*, 2 July 1949.

47. *Houston Informer*, 10 September 1949.

48. Ibid.

49. Ibid., 17 September 1949.

50. Ibid., 22 October 1949.

51. Ibid., 5 November 1949.

52. Ibid., 18 February 1950.

53. Ibid.

54. *Dallas Express*, 1 April 1950.

55. *Houston Informer*, 18 March 1949.

56. Ibid., 15 April 1950.

57. Ibid.

58. Ibid.

59. Ibid.

60. Ibid., 29 April 1950.

61. Ibid., 13 May 1950.

62. Ibid.

63. Ibid.

64. Ibid.

65. Ibid., 13 May 1950.

66. Ibid., 20 May 1950.

67. Ibid., 27 May 1950.

68. Ibid., 10 June 1950.

69. Ibid., 8 July 1950.

70. Ibid.

71. Ibid., 15 July 1950.

72. Ibid., 29 July 1950.

73. Lanctot, *Negro League Baseball*, 354–355.

74. *Houston Informer*, 12 August 1950.

75. Ibid., 9 September 1950.

76. Ibid., 16 September 1950.

77. Ibid.

78. Ibid., 28 October 1950.

79. *Pittsburgh Courier*, 12 January 1952.

CHAPTER 8

1. Bruce Adelson, *Brushing Back Jim Crow: The Integration of Minor-League Base-ball in the American South* (Charlottesville: University Press of Virginia, 1999), 35–36.

2. Richard Kimball, "Beyond the Great Experiment: Integrated Baseball Comes to Indianapolis," *Journal of Sports History* 12, no. 1 (Spring 1985): 146.

3. Adelson, *Brushing Back Jim Crow*, 52.

4. Ibid., 55.

5. Larry Moffi and Jonathan Kronstadt, *Crossing the Line: Black Major Leaguers, 1947–1959* (Jefferson, NC: McFarland and Co., 1994), 95–96.

6. O'Neal, *The Texas League*, 108–109.

7. Moffi and Kronstadt, *Crossing the Line*, 95.

8. Adelson, *Brushing Back Jim Crow*, 35–36.

9. Ibid., 249.

10. Ibid., 255.

11. Jack Davis, "Baseball's Reluctant Challenge: Desegregating Major League Spring Training Sites, 1961–1964," *Journal of Sports History* 19, no. 2 (Summer 1992): 144.

12. Ibid, 145.

13. Riley, *Biographical Encyclopedia*, s.v. "Banks, Ernest."

14. *The Baseball Encyclopedia: The Complete and Definitive Record of Major League Baseball*, 10th ed. (New York: Macmillan, 1996), 1524.

15. Ibid., 1386–1387.

16. Ibid., 770.

17. Riley, *Biographical Encyclopedia*, s.v. "Patterson, Andrew L."

18. Frazier Robinson, *Catching Dreams: My Life in the Negro Baseball Leagues* (Syracuse, NY: Syracuse University Press 1999), 195.

APPENDIX

1. Riley, *Biographical Encyclopedia*.

Bibliography

PRIMARY SOURCES

Newspapers

Austin American-Statesman. 17 January 1998. 2 March 1999.

Chicago Defender. 2, 16 April 1910. 11 April 1914.

Dallas Express. 24 May; 7 June; 23, 30 August 1919. 27 March; 10, 13, 17, 24 April 1920. 12 March; 9, 23 April 1921. 27 May; 9 September 1922. 5 May; 14 July; 18 August 1923. 13 March 1948. 25 March; 14, 28 May; 11, 25 June; 2, 22, 29 July 1949. 1 April 1950.

Houston Informer. 5, 26 March; 14, 21, 28 May; 4 June 1921. 31 March; 7, 21 April; 26 May; 30 June 1923. 5, 26 April 1924. 22 August 1925. 18 September 1926. 19 January; 2, 23 February; 9, 16 March; 6, 20, 27 April; 4, 18, 25 May; 1, 22 June; 13, 20 July; 14, 21, 28 September; 5 October 1929. 29 March; 5, 29 April; 3, 10 May; 2 August; 4 October 1930. 21 February 1931. 13 February 1932. 23 February; 23 March; 6 April; 17, 25 May; 1, 8, 22 June; 6, 13 July 1935. 22 February; 28 March; 2, 30 May; 13, 20 June 1936. 10 March; 7, 28 July; 1, 8 September; 6 October 1945. 5, 23 March 1946. 22 March; 31 May 1947. 13, 20 April; 12 June 1948. 1, 29 January; 26 March; 30 April; 7, 14, 21, 28 May; 11, 25 June; 2, 9 July; 20 August; 3, 10, 17 September; 22 October; 5 November 1949. 18 February; 18 March; 15, 29 April; 13, 20, 27 May; 10 June; 8, 15, 29 July; 12 August; 9, 16 September; 28 October 1950.

Indianapolis Freeman. 12 June; 17 July; 7 August; 18 October; 13, 20 November 1909.
10, 17 September 1910. 7, 14 August; 24 July 1915. 12, 19 May; 4 August 1917. 12
January 1918. 21 February; 20 March 1920.

Pittsburgh Courier. 16, 30 January; 13 February; 9 September; 9 October 1926. 12
January; 12 April 1952.

San Antonio Register. 29 May 1931. 1 April; 24 June; 5 August; 2 September 1932. 2
July; 24 September 1937. 15 May 1936. 31 July 1941. 3 May 1946. 8 July 1949.

Autobiographies and Books

Foster, Andrew. "How to Pitch." *Sol White's History of Colored Base Ball, with Other
Documents on the Early Black Game: 1886–1936.* Edited by Jerry Malloy. Lincoln:
University of Nebraska Press, 1995.

O'Neil, Buck. *I Was Right on Time: My Journey from the Negro Leagues to the Majors.*
New York: Simon and Schuster, 1996.

Robinson, Frazier. *Catching Dreams: My Life in the Negro Baseball Leagues.* Syracuse,
NY: Syracuse University Press, 1999.

Interviews

Eubank, George. Interview by Robert Foster. 9 April 1969. Interview 1A. Tape recording. Southwest Collection. Texas Tech University, Lubbock.

Forkerway, George. Interview by author. 19 August 1999.

Hill, Damon. Interview by David Murrah. 26 June 1975. Interview 1A. Tape recording. Southwest Collection. Texas Tech University, Lubbock.

Priestly, Carlton, and George Wood. Interview by Robert Foster. 9 April 1969. Interview 1A. Tape recording. Southwest Collection. Texas Tech University, Lubbock.

Samuel, Ruben "Jellie." Interview by Patsy Colvert. 5 February 2001. T.L.L. Temple
Memorial Library, Diboll, Texas.

Smith, Dr. Tom. Interview by author. 12 February 1999.

Government Documents

U.S. Bureau of the Census. *Statistical Abstract of the U.S.: 1950.* Washington, DC:
Government Printing Office, 1950.

U.S. Bureau of Commerce. *Negroes in the United States: 1920–1932.* By Charles E.
Hall. Washington, DC: Government Printing Office, 1935.

SECONDARY SOURCES

Books

Adelson, Bruce. *Brushing Back Jim Crow: The Integration of Minor-League Baseball in
the American South.* Charlottesville: University Press of Virginia, 1999.

Barr, Alwyn. *Black Texans: A History of African Americans in Texas, 1528–1995*. Norman: University of Oklahoma Press, 1996.

Baseball Encyclopedia: The Complete and Definitive Record of Major League Baseball. 10th ed. New York: Macmillan, 1996.

Beeth, Howard, and Cary D. Wintz. *Black Dixie: Afro-Texan History and Culture in Houston*. College Station: Texas A&M University Press, 1992.

Brashler, William. *The Story of Negro League Baseball*. New York: Ticknor and Fields, 1994.

Bruce, Janet. *The Kansas City Monarchs: Champions of Black Baseball*. Lawrence: University of Kansas Press, 1985.

Cottrell, Robert Charles. *The Best Pitcher in Baseball: The Life of Rube Foster, Negro League Giant*. New York: New York University Press, 2001.

———. *Blackball, the Black Sox, and the Babe: Baseball's Crucial 1920 Season*. Jefferson, NC: McFarland and Co., 2002.

Debono, Paul. *The Chicago American Giants*. Jefferson, NC: McFarland and Co., 2007.

Douglas, Frederick. *My Bondage and My Freedom*. New York: Dover Publishing, 1969.

Govenar, Alan. *Portraits of Community: African American Photography in Texas*. Austin: Texas State Historical Association, 1996.

Heaphy, Leslie, ed. *Black Baseball and Chicago: Essays on the Players, Teams, and Games of the Negro Leagues' Most Important City*. Jefferson, NC: McFarland and Co., 2006.

———. *The Negro Leagues, 1869–1960*. Jefferson, NC: McFarland and Co., 2003.

Hogan, Lawrence D. *Shades of Glory: The Negro Leagues and the Story of African American Baseball*. Washington, DC: National Geographic, 2006.

Holway, John. *Black Diamonds: Life in the Negro Leagues from the Men Who Lived It*. New York: Stadium Books, 1991.

———. *Blackball Stars: Negro League Pioneers*. New York: Carroll and Graf, 1988.

———. *Voices from the Great Black Baseball Leagues*. New York: De Capo Press, 1975.

Kayser, Tom, and David King. *Baseball in the Lone Star State: The Texas League's Greatest Hits*. San Antonio: Trinity University Press, 2005.

Lanctot, Neil. *Negro League Baseball: The Rise and Ruin of a Black Institution*. Philadelphia: University of Pennsylvania Press, 2004.

Lester, Larry. *Baseball's First Colored World Series: The 1924 Meeting of the Hilldale Giants and Kansas City Monarchs*. Jefferson, NC: McFarland and Co., 2006.

Lomax, Michael E. *Black Baseball Entrepreneurs, 1860–1901: Operating by Any Means Necessary*. Syracuse, NY: Syracuse University Press, 2003.

Luke, Bob. *Willie Wells: "El Diablo" of the Negro Leagues*. Austin: University of Texas Press, 2007.

McNeil, William. *Cool Papas and Double Duties: The All-Time Greats of the Negro Leagues.* Jefferson, NC: McFarland and Co., 2001.

Moffi, Larry, and Jonathan Kronstadt. *Crossing the Line: Black Major Leaguers, 1947–1959.* Jefferson, NC: McFarland and Co., 1994.

Moore, Joseph Thomas. *Pride against Prejudice: The Biography of Larry Doby.* New York: Greenwood Press, 1988.

O'Neal, Bill. *The Texas League: 1888–1987, A Century of Baseball.* Austin: Eakin Press, 1987.

Payne, Darwin. *Big D: Triumph and Troubles of an American Super City in the Twentieth Century.* Dallas: Tree Forks Press, 1994.

Peterson, Robert. *Only the Ball Was White: A History of Legendary Black Players and All-Black Professional Teams.* New York: Oxford University Press, 1970.

Ribowsky, Mark. *A Complete History of the Negro Leagues: 1884 to 1955.* Secaucus, NJ: Carol Publishing Group, 1995.

Riley, James A. *The Biographical Encyclopedia of the Negro Baseball Leagues.* New York: Carroll and Graf Publishers, 1994.

Rogosin, Donn. *Invisible Men: Life in Baseball's Negro Leagues.* New York: Kodansha International, 1983.

Ruck, Rob. *Sandlot Seasons: Sport in Black Pittsburgh.* Urbana: University of Illinois Press, 1993.

Rust, Art, Jr. *Get That Nigger Off the Field: The Oral History of the Negro Leagues.* Brooklyn: Book Mail Services, 1976.

Snyder, Brad. *Beyond the Shadow of the Senators: The Untold Story of the Homestead Grays and the Integration of Baseball.* Chicago: Contemporary Books, 2003.

Tygiel, Jules. *Baseball's Great Experiment: Jackie Robinson and His Legacy.* New York: Vintage Books, 1983.

Ward, Geoffrey C., and Ken Burns. *Baseball: An Illustrated History.* New York: Knopf, 1994.

Withers, Ernest C. *Negro League Baseball.* Edited by Anthony Decaneas. New York: Harry N. Abrams, 2004.

Articles

Bourgeois, Christie L. "Stepping Over Lines: Lyndon Johnson, Black Texans, and the National Youth Administration, 1935–1937." *Southwestern Historical Quarterly* 41, no. 2 (October 1987): 149–172.

Bullock, Steve. "Playing for Their Nation: The American Military and Baseball during World War II." *Journal of Sports History* 27, no. 1 (Spring 2000): 67–89.

Captain, Gwendolyn. "Enter Ladies and Gentlemen of Color: Gender, Sport, and the Ideal of African American Manhood and Womanhood during the Late Nineteenth and Early Twentieth Centuries." *Journal of Sports History* 18, no. 1 (Spring 1991): 81–102.

Carroll, John. "Abner Doubleday Strikes Out Again: The Origin of Baseball in Southeast Texas." *North American Society for Sports History: Proceedings and Newsletter,* 1986, 45–46.

Davis, Jack. "Baseball's Reluctant Challenge: Desegregating Major League Spring Training Sites, 1961–1964." *Journal of Sports History* 19, no. 2 (Summer 1992): 144–162.

Fetter, Henry D. "The Party Line and the Color Line: The American Communist Party, the Daily Worker, and Jackie Robinson." *Journal of Sports History* 28, no. 3 (Fall 2001): 375–402.

Gems, Gerald. "Great Wasn't Good Enough: The Black Sports Experience in Chicago." *North American Society for Sports History: Proceedings and Newsletter,* 1991, 48.

Gerlach, Larry. "Baseball's Other 'Great Experiment': Eddie Klep and the Integration of the Negro Leagues." *Journal of Sports History* 25, no. 3 (Fall 1998): 453–481.

Gorn, Elliott. "Gender, Class, and Sports in Late 19th Century America." *North American Society for Sports History: Proceedings and Newsletter,* 1990, 42.

Glasrud, Bruce A. "William M. McDonald." *Black Leaders: Texans for Their Times.* Edited by Alwyn Barr and Robert A. Calvert. Austin: Texas State Historical Association, 1981.

Hardman, Peggy. "Strickland, Henry." *New Handbook of Texas.* Austin: Texas State Historical Association, 1996.

"Just Deserts." *Texas Highways,* December 2001, 45.

Kimball, Richard Ian. "Beyond the 'Great Experiment': Integrated Baseball Comes to Indianapolis." *Journal of Sports History* 26, no. 1 (Spring 1999): 142–162.

Klainen, Diana J. "White, Julius." *New Handbook of Texas.* Austin: Texas State Historical Association, 1996.

Le Compte, Mary Lou. "Any Sunday in April: The Rise of Sport in San Antonio and the Hispanic Borderlands." *Journal of Sports History* 13, no. 2 (Summer 1986): 128–146.

Lester, Larry. "Andrew 'Rube' Foster: Gem of a Man." *Black Baseball in Chicago: Essays on the Players, Teams, and Games of the Negro Leagues Most Important City.* Edited by Leslie A. Heaphy. Jefferson, NC: McFarland and Co., 2006.

Lomax, Michael. "Black Entrepreneurship in the National Pastime: The Rise of Semiprofessional Baseball in Black Chicago, 1890–1915." *Journal of Sports History* 25, no. 1 (Spring 1998): 43–64.

McKinney, G. B. "Negro Professional Baseball Players in the Upper South in the Gilded Age." *Journal of Sports History* 3, no. 3 (1976): 273–284.

Nathan, Daniel A. "Sugar Ray Robinson, the Sweet Science, and the Politics of Meaning." *Journal of Sports History* 26, no. 1 (Spring 1999): 163–174.

Regalado, Samuel. "Baseball in the Barrios." *North American Society for Sports History: Proceedings and Newsletter,* 1985, 28.

————. "The Battle of San Francisco: The Marichal-Roseboro Affair; August 1965." *North American Society for Sports History: Proceedings and Newsletter*, 1992, 81.

————. "Incarcerated Sport: Nisei Women's Softball and Athletics during Japanese American Internment." *Journal of Sports History* 27, no. 3 (Fall 2000): 431–444.

Riess, Steven A. "The Baseball Magnates and Urban Politics in the Progressive Era: 1895–1920." *Journal of Sports History* 1, no. 1 (1974): 41–62.

Simons, William. "Jackie Robinson and the American Mind: Journalistic Perceptions of the Reintegration of Baseball." *Journal of Sports History* 12, no. 1 (Spring 1985): 39–64.

Wiggins, David K. "Good Times on the Old Plantation: Popular Recreations of Black Slaves in Antebellum South, 1810–1860." *Journal of Sports History* 4, no. 3 (1977): 260–284.

————. "Great Speed but Little Stamina: The Historical Debate over Black Athletic Superiority." *Journal of Sports History* 16, no. 2 (Summer 1989): 158–185.

————. "The Play of Slave Children in the Plantation Communities of the Old South, 1820–1860." *Journal of Sports History* 7, no. 2 (Summer 1980): 21–39.

————. "Wendell Smith, the *Pittsburgh Courier-Journal*, and the Campaign to Include Blacks in Organized Baseball, 1933–1945." *Journal of Sports History* 10, no. 2 (Summer 1983): 5–29.

Museum Exhibits

Play Ball! Texas Baseball. Bob Bullock Texas State History Museum, 14 June 2003–4 January 2004.

Index